The Pursuit.
The work of the Holy
Spirit in evangelism

Mike Mellor

The **Evangelical Movement of Wales** works in both Welsh and English and seeks to help Christians and churches by:

• running children's camps and family conferences

• providing theological training and events for ministers

• running Christian bookshops and a conference centre

• publishing magazines and books

Bryntirion Press is a ministry of EMW. Past issues of EMW magazines and sermons preached at our conferences are available on our web site: www.emw.org.uk

Published by Bryntirion Press, Bryntirion, Bridgend CF31 4DX, Wales, in association with:

EP BOOKS, 1st Floor Venture House, 6 Silver Court, Watchmead, Welwyn Garden City, UK, AL7 1TS
www.epbooks.org

EP BOOKS are distributed in the USA by:
JPL Fulfillment, 3741 Linden Avenue Southeast, Grand Rapids, MI 49548.
sales@jplbooks.com
www.jplbooks.org

MUDIAD EFENGYLAIDD CYMRU
YN GWASANAETHU'R EGLWYS

EVANGELICAL MOVEMENT OF WALES
SERVING THE CHURCH

Commendations

The Bible teaches that only God the Holy Spirit can convict the world of sin, righteousness and judgement. Mike Mellor claims he is looking for those 'desperate enough to be used, empty enough to be filled and humble enough to be led'. It is one of those rare books with a truly transforming message. I dare you to read it without being not only shaken, but stirred.

John Blanchard, Evangelist, Author and Apologist

If you have a passion to share your faith, or are somewhat reluctant to engage in evangelism, I recommend this important book on the subject of the work of the Holy Spirit in evangelism. It pulls together the centrality of His work in both the pursued and the one who seeks to pursue the lost soul. Or, as Mike puts it, 'Being sensitive to the Holy means being eagerly listening for His voice in order to do His will'. How we need more of the Holy Spirit's work in our lives, to have the same compassion for the lost and desire to see their eyes opened to the glory of God's saving grace!

Trevor Dickerson, National Field Director of Outreach UK

I commend this excellent book to you without reservation. As an author, I am almost lost for words in commending this book. Exciting. A compelling read. Challenging. Searching. Anecdotal, yet profoundly biblical. Balanced, in that salvation is God's work but He sovereignly chooses to use our lives, our words and our prayers. A necessary and contemporary book. All I can do is to urge you to buy and read the book. Only then will you endorse what I am saying and benefit from it!

Eryl Davies, Consulting Editor of *Evangelical Magazine* and former Principal of Evangelical Theological College of Wales (now Union).

Do you remember the thrill when you first sensed the Holy Spirit 'nudging' you to witness to someone about the Lord Jesus? Has it been a long time since it last happened? Well, The Pursuit is a reliable guide for understanding how the Holy Spirit wants to 'partner' with us to fulfil His sovereign purposes in saving souls. Theologically robust, scripturally supported, thoroughly practical, peppered with quotable quotations and personal testimony, this is a page-turner and a must-read for every believer.

Steven Green, UK Director of Mobilisation and Church Relations for ReachAcross—Helping Muslims Follow Jesus

Who's at work in evangelism? If not by belief, then by behaviour we often answer 'us!' That can only lead to discouragement. Mike, with his very warm and engaging style, shows us that the HolySpirit, ourselves and even the devil are all involved and that is such a liberating truth. This book has a wonderful mix of personal anecdotes, stories from church history and, of course, biblical examples which together with solid teaching on the work of the Holy Spirit will serve to enthuse, encourage and equip us for the great task of evangelism.

Tim Howlett, Executive Officer, United Beach Missions/Young Life

Mike Mellor writes with an evangelist's heart and passion. In a book packed with numerous anecdotes, historical references, theological reflections and interleaved with his own thrilling story, Mike urges each one to take up the challenge of sharing Christ. Your heart will be warmed, your mind challenged and your zeal stirred.

Andy Paterson, Mission Director, Fellowship of Independent Evangelical Churches

I knew Mike before he was a Christian when there were times he was so intoxicated with alcohol that he couldn't grip a pen to write, nor could he string two sentences together that made any sense! But God has done great things for him and has saved and changed him. And now, by God's grace, he writes a book that is both gripping and makes perfect sense. It is a stirring and inspiring book with a healthy balance of honest realism and Spirit-filled expectation. It is a clear and urgent call to evangelistic action and a sound acknowledgment that we depend upon a Sovereign God in all that action. Mike writes fast and you find yourself racing along turning the pages, except that its contents are so serious that you have to make yourself stop, think, and consider the force of truth you are reading. May God use this book as a spark to light a fire that may have gone out in our lives, and may the fruit of this book be a vast army of Christians who make witnessing part of their regular way of life.

Paul Pease, Pastor of Hook Evangelical Church, Surrey

Dedication

To Roger Carswell

His passionate, joyful, infectious zeal, his warm, winsome evangelistic preaching, his faithfulness to Scripture and his unswerving determination to reach the lost have been a humbling challenge, yet constant spur to me the past thirty years or so.

Contents

Acknowledgments

It takes twenty years to make a sermon, because it takes twenty years to make the man. The true sermon is a thing of life.

E. M. Bounds

This book was written in months but took many years to produce. As a result I am indebted to so many people past and present, but here am able to name just a few. When in Bible College in South Wales many years ago, I would often escape the hubbub of student life by slipping out to a small lecture room in which were kept all the Christian biographies. I would sit alone, basking in the atmosphere of that fragrant, sacred space, alone with my 'friends'. Although separated by many centuries in some cases, they were a present encouragement, as I felt the same heavenly pressure to serve the same Saviour, in the same glorious work as they. A number of them will appear in this book, so I would firstly like to acknowledge my gratitude to that 'cloud of witnesses' (Hebrews 12:1) who have run their race, but continue to urge you and me on to heroic efforts for Jesus in this, our generation.

And then, my sincere gratitude to the following saints who are still 'running with perseverance':

Paul Pease, whose 'beautiful feet' brought the good news of salvation to this 'hopeless case'.

Peter Williams, from whose lips I first heard passionate preaching week by week as a new-born believer, and whose wise counsel I received during the early stages of my call to ministry.

Jonny Raine, whose request to me to write a short article for the *Evangelical Magazine* was the spark that fanned into a flame and then into a book.

Laura Thomas, our eldest author-daughter, whose gracious badgering convinced me to continue writing when doubts flooded in.

Bill James, for agreeing to scan my early manuscript for heresy, and then being willing to accompany me to the stake, if charged.

Eryl Davies, for his encouragement and wise suggestions, which I have been only too willing to implement.

Linda Baynham, who was a key worker in our South Wales and Covent Garden churches, for her characteristically efficient and eagle-eyed editing.

George Verwer, not only for his more than generous Foreword, but for his life of breath-taking faith and vision.

Gwen, my dear, long-suffering wife, who could never have imagined what would be entailed when she agreed to love me 'for better, for worse...'

Foreword

Mike is not just someone writing another book, but a person of action who is putting what he writes into practice. I suggest you don't read this book unless you want the Holy Spirit to move you into action.

As I think of this book, five words, or biblical principles, come to mind that I think will really help you in your own walk with Jesus:

1. **The Ministry of the Holy Spirit.** This is one of the main features of the book, to show how the Holy Spirit can lead us and guide us and help us in evangelism.

2. **Balance.** Over the years I have seen so much extremism practised under the claim that it's the Holy Spirit. So I am happy that this book has a real practical balance, especially of what the Holy Spirit does and does not do.

3. **Realistic expectation.** Over the years I have seen people, even in our own movement, Operation Mobilisation, praying wild, unrealistic prayers and then launching into evangelism expecting huge numbers of conversions. Often disappointments soon come and this sometimes leads to disunity among those trying to work together. Mike does not hesitate to speak into this in a Scriptural way.

4. **Research.** Mike has done a lot of reading and research to give us this book. He has gone to great lengths to read about some of the great evangelists of history so that we can learn from them. I am sure this book can be used as a study manual for those wanting to grow and learn more in this area.

5. **Holy Spirit action.** The Word of God is so clear that we are to be doers of the Word, not just hearers. In fact, it is very strong in saying that if we are only hearing (this includes, for sure, reading) and not doing, then we are deceiving ourselves.

I suggest you pray your way through this powerful book rather than just read it. I hope you will get a few extra copies for friends and that in the end there will be people coming to Jesus as a result of this book.

George Verwer DD
Founder of Operation Mobilisation and former Director

Introduction—The Lost Wonder

There are so many aspects of the Christian life that blow our minds when we are first converted. Lofty things, supernatural things: the reality of God's love, the power of the gospel, the wonder of the cross, the beauty of forgiveness, the privilege of Christian fellowship, the relevance of the Bible, the glories of heaven, the horrors of hell—these being just a few of the new and astounding discoveries that break in upon our lives. But, somehow, with the passing of time or perhaps the pressures and demands of life, we shamefully relegate them to the realm of the ordinary, the routine and, dare we admit it, the mundane. The initial wonder of being accepted and freely pardoned by the Maker of the universe, whose love and laws we had trampled over for years, but who had lovingly bought, sought and then brought us into His heavenly family, has somehow evaporated. One of these diminished wonders is the incredible fact that, as Christians, we each are indwelt by this glorious Being and have been enlisted to serve and represent Him all our days here on earth. A daunting prospect? Yes, but we have been given the promise of His personal presence with us in this. Take those heart-melting words of the Lord Jesus: 'Surely I am with you always...' As a brand new Christian, I was so overwhelmed by this magnificent reality that I could hardly wait to leave work to get into my car alone with Him. Irreverent though it might seem, I felt as though Jesus was sitting beside me in the passenger seat as I drove. Perhaps you have known similar precious times.

Of the countless possible facets of this life of faith we could consider, the particular emphasis in these pages will be that, just as the Saviour came on a mission 'to seek and to save the lost', we too are to have His heart of compassion and, filled with His Spirit, are to daily seek after those who are, tragically, doing their utmost to avoid being found. My deep concern is that so many Christians are content to live their lives while missing a vital dimension and dynamic to their faith: the joyful sharing of the gospel, which subsequently serves to re-kindle the personal inner flame of devotion that so can so easily burn low.

My aim is twofold: firstly that we will be convinced biblically that the Holy Spirit is the Director of all evangelism and mission and, secondly, that the joyful, at times euphoric experience of being led by the Lord in eyeball-to-eyeball, heartbeat-to-heartbeat evangelism, might become a regular way of life. For some, it might be entering for the first time into the 'romance' of seeing what God can do for the one who seeks to walk humbly and expectantly with Him. For others, it may be we recapture something of the wonder that has been lost through that wearying unbelief that 'makes the world a moral desert, where no divine footsteps are heard, where no angels ascend and descend, where no living hand adorns the fields, feeds the birds of heaven or regulates events.'[1]

My prayer is that our hearts may be ignited with the holy flame which has burned intensely in the hearts of Christ-possessed men and women through the ages who were desperate enough to be used, empty enough to be filled and humble enough to be led.

> Father, forgive me for being so ordinary while claiming to know so extraordinary a God.
>
> Jim Elliot

1 The Pursuit

I fled Him, down the nights and down the days;
I fled Him, down the arches of the years;
I fled Him, down the labyrinthine ways
Of my own mind; and in the midst of tears
I hid from Him, and under running laughter.
Up vistaed hopes I sped;
And shot, precipitated,
Adown Titanic glooms of chasmed fears,
From those strong Feet that followed, followed after.
But with unhurrying chase,
And unperturbed pace,
Deliberate speed, majestic instancy,
They beat—and a Voice beat ...

'The Hound of Heaven' (Francis Thompson, 1859–1907)

The poem 'The Hound of Heaven' was written by the English poet Francis Thompson and graphically tells the tale of how we all, by human nature, flee Adam-like from the God who loves us and earnestly pursues us in order to rescue, redeem and reconcile us. The words stream dramatically from a tortured heart, the author's personal life being one punctuated by failure, addiction and sorrow until his premature death at the age of forty-eight. But throughout his turbulent years, Thompson felt the hot breath of this 'holy hound' relentlessly in pursuit and recorded in his poem the heart-thumping experience which he so keenly felt.

The flight

Of course, we must start at the beginning. After that first and fatal act of rebellion in the Garden, the two insurgents, overwhelmed with guilt and shame, run and hide. We can only imagine what avalanche of darkness must have descended upon the pair in an instant. What colossal sense of horror, loss and regret they felt as the madness and irrationality of sin in its grotesque and diverse manifestations began to break upon them in the twinkling of an eye.

Rather than running towards the God they loved, begging for forgiveness and reconciliation, they run from him, seeking to escape the presence and company of the One whom, just minutes before, they had revelled in. The air is thick with despair. Surely there is no possibility of a way back from this?

Nevertheless, they are sought immediately by their gracious, omniscient God who, knowing exactly where the guilty pair are, addresses Adam earnestly and tenderly with the rhetorical question, 'Where are you?' (Genesis 3:9). It is this great Seeker of souls who later would be revealed in His richest form as the Good Shepherd.

The vitally important point to grasp is that it is God taking the initiative, God making the first move, God doing the seeking. It seems that all world religions, apart from Christianity, emphasise man's seeking after God. Only the Bible reveals the God who seeks after guilty men and women. Millennia have passed, but the condition remains the same for the human race, the children of those first parents. We are all 'on the run' from our Maker. Our personal stories may differ, the escape routes we take may vary, but we are all prodigals and in desperate need of being pursued. The Apostle Paul drives this terrible truth home, underscoring the point made by the Old Testament Psalmist, 'There is no-one righteous, not even one; there is no-one who understands; there is no-one who seeks God.' (Romans 3:10–11). Of ourselves we have no desire for God and rely wholly upon His merciful desire for us. So we fugitives run, hide and escape through an array of frantic scenarios during our lifetime. But there is a Pursuer! 'As the hound follows the hare, never ceasing in its running, ever drawing nearer in the chase, with unhurrying and unperturbed pace, so does God follow the fleeing soul by His Divine grace.'[2]

Although possibly aware of God's loving interest in us, the God-avoider flees, believing the devil's lie that submitting to God will mean forfeiting a life of happiness, which always eludes us anyhow, for one of tight-laced toil and joyless drudgery. Prolific Oxford academic and author C.S. Lewis famously captures this 'great escape' as he recalls his own conversion:

> You must picture me alone in that room in Magdalen, night after night, feeling, whenever my mind lifted even for a second from my work, the steady, unrelenting approach of Him whom I so earnestly desired not to meet. That which I greatly feared had at last come upon me. In the Trinity Term of 1929 I gave in, and admitted that God was God, and knelt and prayed: perhaps, that night, the most dejected and reluctant convert in all England. I did not then see what is now the most shining and obvious thing; the Divine humility which will accept a convert even on such terms. The Prodigal Son at least walked home on his own feet. But who can duly adore that Love which will open the high gates to a prodigal who is brought in kicking, struggling, resentful, and darting his eyes in every direction for a chance of escape?[3]

Futile pursuit

Of course, attempting to escape from an omniscient, omnipotent God is the height of folly, because 'Nothing in all creation is hidden from God's sight. Everything is uncovered and laid bare before the eyes of him to whom we must give account.' (Hebrews 4:13). The Psalmist King David was only too aware of this also:

> Where can I go from your Spirit?
> Where can I flee from your presence?
> If I go up to the heavens, you are there;
> If I make my bed in the depths, you are there.
> If I rise on the wings of the dawn,
> If I settle on the far side of the sea,
> even there your hand will guide me,
> your right hand will hold me fast.
> If I say, 'Surely the darkness will hide me
> and the light become night around me,'
> even the darkness will not be dark to you;
> the night will shine like the day,
> for darkness is as light to you.
> (Psalm 139:7–12)

Nothing is hidden from God—and He knows where you live! Thankfully, we have a loving, sovereign Lord who places each of us in exactly the right place, at the right time, with the sole aim that we might seek Him! 'From one man he made all the nations, that they should inhabit the whole earth; and he marked out   their appointed times in history and the boundaries of their lands. God did this so that they would seek him and perhaps reach out for him and find him, though he is not far from any one of us' (Acts 17:26–27).

Conscience

Pierre-Joseph Proudhon, the nineteenth-century French economist, remarked brazenly, 'The first duty of free and intelligent man is to chase the idea of God out of his conscience incessantly.'[4] But he was naively unaware of one vital factor—that the human conscience is given by God! Every human has been gifted with an inner 'moral monitor'. When King Solomon rebuked Shimei for shamefully wronging his father David, he cuts through any possible defence the reckless ranter may have offered, saying, 'You know in your heart all the wrong you did ...' (1 Kings 2:44). The Apostle Paul, speaking of Gentiles who had not been privileged to have God's written revelation as the Jews had, writes, 'They show that the requirements of the law are written on their hearts, their consciences also bearing witness, and their thoughts sometimes accusing them and at other times even defending them' (Romans 2:15).

Bible commentator Matthew Henry calls the conscience 'That candle of the Lord that was not put out.' Puritan Thomas Brooks describes its role in each person as 'God's preacher in the bosom'. The bottom line is that none of us can plead 'not guilty'. Evangelist Ray Comfort affirms,

> The word 'con-science' means 'with knowledge.' The conscience is the 'headline' warning of sin; the Scriptures give 'the fine print'. None of us can say that we don't know it's wrong to lie, steal, murder, or commit adultery; that knowledge is written in large print on our heart. However, in the Scriptures we see the true nature of sin: that God requires truth even in the inward parts (Psalm 51:6). The fine print reveals that lust is adultery of the heart, hatred is murder of the heart, fibs are bearing false witness ...[5]

The Holy Spirit convicts

Although the gospel is 'good news', it is in fact bad news to begin with! Here we are, on the run, trying to be happy without God and... 'Ouch!'—'What was that?' We fail to recognise it at the beginning, but the Hound of Heaven is on our track. The One 'we so earnestly desired not to meet', as

Lewis drolly put it, is at work through the Holy Spirit. And it is far from comfortable!

Before going to the cross, Jesus is preparing His handful of dim disciples for their task of world mission. How daunting! But He encourages them by informing them that when He leaves it is not down to them to convince an unbelieving world about Him, but that He will send 'another Counsellor', the Holy Spirit. 'When he comes, he will prove the world to be in the wrong about sin and righteousness and judgment' (John 16:8).

It will be the work of the Holy Spirit to convict, that is, to 'prove wrong', 'lay bare', 'expose'. He will come into this world of denial, where most of its inhabitants are seeking to live for themselves and not for God, for time, rather than eternity, and lovingly intrude, disturb and interrupt their plans, dreams and philosophies. It is no wonder that when the first Christians, a bunch of nobodies, approached a town, panic gripped the people and the cry went up, 'These men who have caused trouble all over the world have now come here' (Acts 17:6).

James Montgomery Boice, writing about the amazing growth and impact of the early church, comments:

> Humanly speaking, it had nothing going for it. It had no money, no proven leaders, no technological tools for propagating the gospel. And it faced enormous obstacles. It was utterly new, it taught truths that were incredible to an unregenerate world. It was subject to the most intense hatreds and persecutions. Yet, as Luke records its growth in this document (Acts), it spread from Jerusalem (an obscure corner of the world) to Rome, the world's capital—all within a lifetime of the first generation of believers.[6]

It is no gospel that teaches people they can 'slip into' Christianity without there being any radical change in the new convert's life. 'If anyone is in Christ, the new creation has come: the old has gone, the new is here!' (2 Corinthians 5:17). Everything is turned upside down, every part of the life is affected. We instinctively know it is that way; this is the reason we are on the run!

Alice Cooper, who has enjoyed his 'wild man of rock' reputation for decades, declared in an interview for *The Sunday Times Magazine*, 'It's the most rebellious thing I've ever done! Drinking beer is easy. Trashing your hotel room is easy. But being a Christian—that is a tough call! That's real rebellion!'[7] Some may be quick to judge the veteran rocker's profession of faith, but it is plain to see he has grasped the vital fact that the Christian life is radical, 'rebellious', truly counter-culture. It is surrendering your life to Someone you have never seen, trusting in a Man who claimed equality to God yet was executed publicly in shame, who Christians claim is now alive. Yet coming, 'kicking, struggling, resentful' to the wonderful discovery, eventually, that it is all absolutely true!

What is impossible with man ...

No-one could have been more surprised than myself, journeying to work as a hopeless alcoholic one morning and returning home the same day in tears of joy, knowing without any shadow of doubt that God knew all about me, yet loved me. Knowing that Christ had died, yet had risen—and that my life would never be the same again. The hard part was arriving home and trying to explain to a near despairing wife what had happened. She had heard all the stories of 'turning over a new leaf' before. However, there was no doubting the reality of this change, as a week later this once bleary-eyed 'thing' was now bright-eyed, sober and attending a prayer meeting! Just days before, he was surrounded by a bunch of the most undesirable characters any decent person would seek to avoid, yet now, he's in the midst of a small gathering of elderly, bun-wearing ladies, feeling strangely at home and thinking to himself, 'these are now my people!'

We must never lose sight of the wonder of Christian conversion. It is *always* a Holy Spirit-wrought miracle. If someone is from a Christian home, nurtured in a godly atmosphere where prayer and Bible reading are the norm and their experience is far from dramatic, may they not for one moment forget that the same supernatural power was required in their instance too. This fact was impressed upon me convincingly one evening in a prison in the South of England. Before my opportunity to preach, it was the pattern to have one of the visiting team share a word of personal testimony and this night it was Ben's turn.

The son of a pastor, he had trusted Christ as his Saviour at the age of seven. Standing to speak, this young man, now in his late teens, nervously eyed his audience, a group of cynical, world-weary men whose rolling eyes spoke volumes as they waited for this fresh-faced, sheltered stripling to address them. As Ben recounted to them the details of his faith, their scornful looks must have been hard for him to take.

But something happened that turned the meeting around. One of the men, whose face eloquently conveyed the story of his turbulent life, interrupted, saying in a token London accent, "ere, I ged it mate! You're standin' 'ere telling us 'ow God 'as 'elped and guided you, and 'ere's me wiv an addiction problem, a string of broken relationships and in a minute I gotta go back to a prison cell!' He did indeed 'ged it'. He understood clearly that by the Spirit's power—and only by the Spirit's power—a person can live a godly life in an ungodly world, travelling the road of life enjoying God's blessing all along the journey.

You see, Ben has a great testimony. Mine is a bad testimony: having to speak of how I needed rescuing from a mess of my own making because I didn't live as God prescribed. This is a testimony to avoid having. Ben's testimony is just how it should be: Age seven, loving Jesus. Age seventeen, loving Jesus. Age seventy, loving Jesus. All through life until final breath, loving Jesus. Surely this is when the church is most effective—when each and every believer is a courageous, yet gracious, witness and 'gossips the gospel' by life and lip, sharing simply, 'what the Lord has done for me'. In this way the Holy Spirit convicts unbelievers of their need of a Saviour.

The counter-culture lifestyle of a Christian is always an enigma to the unsaved, producing discomfort and conviction. It is due to the sheer love and patience of God alone that in the momentous days in which we are living He has not wrapped the whole thing up. But, 'not wanting anyone to perish, but everyone to come to repentance' (2 Peter 3:9), He is pursuing sinners 'down the nights and down the days ... down the arches of the years ... down the labyrinthine ways'. However, the question is, 'Who will be willing to be used by the Hound of Heaven in His relentless pursuit of 'the sons of Adam and daughters of Eve'?'

2 The Pursuers

Down in the human heart, crushed by the tempter.
Feelings lie buried that grace can restore;
Touched by a loving heart, wakened by kindness.
Chords that were broken will vibrate once more.
Frances Crosby, from the hymn 'Rescue the Perishing'

Touched by a loving heart! Whose heart? Divine or human? It has to be God's, of course, to result in any deep and eternal blessing. But surely it is about the divine heart beating and working through human hearts that are moved by His love? Bible teacher and author Warren Wiersbe rightly says that 'Ministry takes place when divine resources meet human needs through loving channels to the glory of God.'[8]

We rejoice in the incarnation, that 'the Word became flesh and made his dwelling among us' (John 1:14). God clothed Himself in 'the rags of our humanity' in order to save us (Philippians 2:6–11; Hebrews 10:5–7). But He has then chosen to bring about His purposes of salvation for His world chiefly through using those saved ones. Angels would be a poor substitute for this work, as they have never experienced the bitterness of sin and the joy and gratitude of sins freely forgiven.

Can there be a higher calling in all the world than being used as an agent in changing a person's hell to heaven? The incredible fact is that any of us can be involved in the lifting, healing and restoration of our fellow strugglers in life—*if* we are willing to be obedient to the voice of the Holy Spirit as He moves, directs and equips us.

Love and kindness

The hymns of Fanny Crosby may sound a little antiquated to our modern ears, but she sounded strong martial tones that we today are in danger of losing. In her deeply emotive hymn 'Rescue the Perishing', she brings out two qualities that have a unique restorative power: love and kindness. It is these two qualities that I think are essential above all others in this 'rescue' work—although it is, of course, the Saviour who is doing this through those seeking to be sensitive to the Holy Spirit, 'For the Son of Man came to seek and to save the lost' (Luke 19:10). Ultimately it has to be His loving heart and His kindness, as such shallow hearts as ours can never contain the depths of loving kindness required for such a task.

The value of one

We live in a high-powered, success-driven, numbers-conscious age, which affects us much more than we would care to admit. Perhaps our greatest need is to grasp just how precious one immortal soul is. A deep conviction of the 'value of one' will keep us from being cold, professional and aloof and will burn within us a warmth, transparency and consistency. Practically, it will deliver us from the inevitable depression and discouragement that come from playing the numbers game.

Phillips Brooks, describing the way the gospels reveal the value Jesus placed upon each precious soul, writes of 'the intense value the Saviour always set upon the souls for which he lived and died. It shines in everything he says and does. It looks out from his eyes when they are happiest and when they are saddest. It trembles in the most loving consolations, and thunders in the most passionate rebukes which come from his lips.'[9]

When we are gripped by such a view of 'the ones', it gives us a motivation that delivers us from the guilt-driven snare of going through the motions, whether on a personal level or, in a local church context, merely ticking the evangelism box on the church evangelism calendar. We must fight to keep this conviction that 'the ones' are precious; they mattered to Jesus as He walked this earth and they matter to Him now.

The Saviour's love for sinners climaxes on the cross, where we see the King preaching forgiveness from His throne of wood for the thief at His side and the mockers before His face. God never sees crowds as a mass of faces, but each one is known and loved, as they journey through life with their hopes, fears and burdens. 'For Christ's love compels us, because we are convinced that one died for all, and therefore all died.' (2 Corinthians. 5:14).

When serving in Central London, I frequently had to rebuke myself for pushing past people, seeing them simply as obstacles to be avoided on my way to 'ministry'. Travelling on the Underground, a place where eye contact is resolutely avoided, I would force myself to look into each face and seek to assess what their life might be. Is this a businessman consumed by work, care and deadlines? A teenage girl who has fled to the big city to escape the restrictions of home? A lonely elderly person, simply a statistic, who will leave this life unloved and unmissed?

C. S. Lewis greatly helps us to be aware that 'the dullest and most uninteresting person you talk to may one day be a creature which, if you saw it now, you would be strongly tempted to worship, or else a horror and a corruption such as you now meet, if at all, only in a nightmare... There are no ordinary people. You have never talked to a mere mortal... it is immortals whom we joke with, work with, marry, snub and exploit—immortal horrors or everlasting splendours...'[10]

No ordinary people

Whilst speaking with people, we need to look into their faces and be charged with the same compassion that surged through the being of our Saviour when confronted with the wealthy young man. We read that 'Jesus looked at him and loved him.' (Mark 10:21).

George Dempster was a man who, in his passionate desire to reach others for Christ, realised the necessity of keeping 'in step with the Spirit'. This respected minister would put on some old, ragged clothes and hang out with the homeless at all hours of the day and night, in order to reach them. Billy Graham's wife, Ruth, wrote of him, 'It was the high point of my life—meeting this small, unimpressive little man with his twinkling eyes ... Thousands were packing the Haringey Arena in London each night to hear my husband preach. Mr. Dempster was out there in the streets and alleyways all hours of the night and early mornings searching for those in need of a Saviour, who would never show up at an evangelistic meeting.'[11]

I personally am totally committed to the proclamation of the gospel through preaching, but there is something special about sharing the Good News in a one-on-one setting. I wholeheartedly agree with D.L. Moody when he states, 'The best sermons are those where one man is the preacher and one man is the congregation'.

We are able to find out just where that 'one' is in their thinking and sensitively start where they are. Although we have a 'one size fits all' gospel, we must adapt and apply the message to the 'congregation' before us. I will use a completely different approach to the bright young university student before me, who is extolling the virtues of Richard Dawkins, than to the broken young woman struggling with drug addiction. The great constant with each and every one, however, is that 'love and kindness' must drive all that we say, especially the hard truths that are contained in the gospel.

Message, manner, motivation

It has been said, rather mischievously, that there are essentially two reasons why people are not Christians:

1. They have never met a Christian.
2. They have met a Christian.

Not everyone is an evangelist, but everyone is called to be a witness for Christ (Acts 1:8, 8:4). This may be stating the obvious, but it is a glorious fact. When speaking of the God who is invisible, we who know Him are somehow (we will see just 'how' later) all commissioned to convey something of the truth and beauty of our Saviour in word and deed. Every follower of Jesus, whether aware of it or not, whether vocal or non-vocal, is a witness.

The question is, 'What kind of witness are we?' Joel Beeke states: 'To be a witness of the Christian faith is complex. It involves the whole lifestyle of the individual. We testify by our silences, our facial expressions, our reactions when we are challenged, and by our conversation ... True witnessing should demonstrate the fruit of the Spirit in "love, joy, peace, patience, gentleness, goodness, faith, meekness and self-control." We need to be aware that we are always being watched and that our lives are constantly 'speaking'. 'The Christian is a walking sermon. They preach far more than a minister does, for they preach all week long', said the Bishop of Liverpool, J.C. Ryle.

Our world teaches so often that there can be a dichotomy between public and private life, a dichotomy played out frequently in the lives of politicians or celebrities. But this can never be so for the one who places such dependence on the Holy Spirit. Character matters and we dare not view evangelism as an impersonal process detached from the moral life of the one engaged in it. Perhaps this is the reason I personally have a strong dislike for the word 'evangelism'! You might think that's pretty unfortunate for someone who has spent so many years trying to do it!

I appreciate we do need to have terms and labels, but my problem here is that we are making something which should be natural seem contrived and manufactured, instead of it being an unconscious overflow of a life. We know only too well what it is to be switched off or even irritated by the pressurising sales people we try to avoid as they bombard us in all manner of ways with their products. The pushier and oilier they are, the less real impact they have.

I am all for training Christians to share the gospel; let us make every effort to be as well-equipped as we can. But there is an external and an internal involved here. Perhaps never in the church's history have we been so well equipped with knowledge—the external—having access, thanks to the internet, to a wealth of instruction and teaching. But there is something lacking internally. We are strong on message but sadly lacking when it comes to motivation and desire.

Soul lover, soul winner

While I do not wish to hark back to the past—'Do not say, "Why were the old days better than these?"' (Ecclesiastes 7:10), —there have been periods when every Christian was encouraged to be a soul-winner. If a person was 'born again', they, motivated by the same love that had taken hold of them, automatically went to seek others for Christ. Admittedly, it was a daunting prospect for a new Christian, but there was something noble and courageous about it—a 'baptism of fire' which would leave an indelible mark upon the fledgling disciple. The problem is that we live in an 'asbestos' type culture, which has us in a fire-quenching pincer grip.

Firstly, we are called to live for Christ in a smug postmodern atmosphere. Simple faith in Christ for salvation is considered to be an extremely simplistic message, one which any thinking person could never seriously be expected to embrace. We are embarrassed into silence. Secondly, ours is a multicultural society and there is increasing pressure upon us to 'tread softly', carefully avoiding any accusation of being labelled 'extremist'. We are bullied into silence.

As a result, we are being pressurised into becoming so compliant that a certain 'bite' is disappearing from our evangelism and it is in danger of becoming rather bland. 'Nice', but bland! We have no end of evangelistic programmes on the church calendar, but Christians can be involved in them without any healthy 'eyeball-to-eyeball, heart-to-heart' sharing of their faith and as a result fail to develop that gritty cross-carrying type of discipleship, which surely is true discipleship.

Please don't misunderstand me. I am not appealing for that brash, insensitive "'ave it!' approach which is always obnoxious wherever it appears, but rather for that fragrant, bold 'taking on the world' spirit that we see so clearly in those weak, infant churches in the New Testament. Our world is desperate to see a people enthralled by the God they profess to believe in and lovingly abandoned to His cause.

The controversial American Episcopalian Robert Capon wrote searchingly that, as Christians, we had 'lost our astonishment'. He laid the blame for this at the feet of the

church for 'hiding the astonishment of the gospel'.[12] Fired by
this thought, speaker and writer Mike Yaconelli penned, 'If
Christianity is simply about being nice, I'm not interested.
What happened to radical Christianity, the un-nice brand of
Christianity that turned the world upside-down? I'm ready for
a Christianity that "ruins" my life, which captures my heart
and makes me uncomfortable. I want to be filled with an
astonishment which is so captivating that I am considered
wild and unpredictable and, well, dangerous. Yes, I want to be
"dangerous" to a dull and boring religion. I want a faith that is
considered "dangerous" by our predictable and monotonous
culture.'[13]

If it is true, as many tell us, that Western culture has
almost become 'first century', then surely it is time to imitate
the raw, daring faith of those who, despite pressure not to
speak in the name of Jesus, replied, 'we cannot help speaking
about what we have seen and heard' (Acts 4:20). It was said
of the infant church in Thessalonica, 'The Lord's message
rang out from you' and 'your faith in God has become known
everywhere' (1 Thessalonians 1:8).

Nothing to lose

These guys had no reputation to lose. They were nobodies and
rejoiced in it. If they were to die, it would certainly not be of
dignity! That irrepressible apostle, Paul, seemed even to delight
in his titles, 'scum of the earth' and 'garbage of the world' (1
Corinthians. 4:13) and no doubt ensured that both were listed
on his CV! In comparison, we think we may win a lost world by
the quality of our website, literature, buildings, etc. In all these,
we should aim to be the best (let us never think that being
shoddy, cheapskate or antiquated is 'spiritual'), but if our trust
is in them, we shall depart from that vital New Testament

authenticity and power and may not even realise it in our blur of organisational activity.

Evangelism and revival

In his thrilling book *Grace, Grit and Gumption*, Geraint Fielder speaks of the evangelistic fervour in South Wales that was to burst into the remarkable 1904 Revival. He entices us to read by issuing this mouth-watering challenge: 'Can you imagine a revival in today's overstressed, over-worked, pleasure-seeking obsessed, unchurched society? It can happen! Discover how in this encouraging story of a dramatic turnaround that changed a whole area of Wales.'[14]

Evangelism is not revival, neither can evangelism produce revival. You can organise, advertise and supervise evangelism, but you can do none of those things with revival. It is always a sovereign work of God, which He begins, controls and ends. Yet, I am personally convinced that there is an inseparable connection between the two. It is the Holy Spirit who quickens and constrains men and women to seek God more earnestly in prayer and compels them to go out seeking to reach the unsaved masses. And even though God should withhold from sending national revival, when we make seeking the lost in our Saviour's name a priority, there will be a personal one. Regardless of how others are impacted, something happens to ourselves when we speak about Jesus, because we are then in one accord with all that the Holy Spirit, the Hound of Heaven is about—lovingly, patiently pursuing men and women:

> With unhurrying chase,
> And unperturbèd pace,
> Deliberate speed, majestic instancy

The Holy Spirit is the Director of all evangelism and mission and is ever seeking to fill us that we may be His 'clothing' in The Pursuit, leading us into appointed situations where we stand thrilled, in open-mouthed awe, exclaiming, 'This is of God!' But we need to be convinced that it is God who is to receive the praise through rescued, redeemed and reclaimed lives. He will not share His glory with another (Isaiah 42:8). Our motives matter. We need to ask the Holy Spirit to search our hearts, because He is looking for those who simply are desperate enough to be used, empty enough to be filled and humble enough to be led.

3 Crisis people

Father, make of me a crisis man. Bring those I contact to decision. Let me not be a milepost on a single road; make me a fork, that men must turn one way or another on facing Christ in me.

Jim Elliot[15]

'Wild, unpredictable, dangerous!' Would those words used by Mike Yaconelli describe you? Your church? I suspect that most of us have successfully avoided the snare of fanaticism, but if we are completely honest we find ourselves struggling to escape the doctrinal straight-jacket of conformity, respectability and predictability that is waiting for us as we stand in safety at the other end of the doctrinal spectrum.

Of course, we all have our blind spots and, as in every group of believers, you doubtless would have found plenty wrong with those infant Christians as we read about them in the Book of Acts. Yet I'm sure the words 'bland' and 'rut' would be missing in any list of their faults. Whilst striving to be winsome and sensitive (and we must), we need somehow to regain the rawness that characterised our new-born devotion to the despised Nazarene. I confess that I find Capon's and Yaconelli's words pierce my own soul and am convicted by my loss of the 'astonishment' I had when first captivated by the love of Christ—an astonishment that just could not be concealed.

Gwen was a singer and as she prepared for work one night she found herself deeply concerned and perplexed by the sudden change in her husband who had long battled addiction. Although relieved by the way he had now become a responsible husband and father, she was secretly afraid of the strange power that had possessed him, his attendance at a church and the new set of friends he had. Strangely, she felt even more of an outsider than before, when he was absent from home spending hours on end with his booze buddies. She played the first set of her gig that night and, as she sat with the rest of the band in the bar during their break, the topic of conversation turned to her husband who was notorious on the music scene. Questions flowed that Gwen was unable to answer:

'What on earth has happened to Mike?'

'Is it true he's got religious mania?'

'It's all a joke, right?'

Then, oddly, Gwen found herself defending him, whereas to his face she questioned, even argued, with him. 'Well, to be honest, I can't fault him. He's loving and reliable, home for meals, playing with the kids. In fact, he's the husband I always wanted!' Then Jonny, the drummer, quipped, 'If you ask me, you'll be one of those Christians next!' 'Oh, no! Not me', Gwen shot back.

Later that night, as she drove home in her car alone, it was as though a voice within asked her gently, 'Gwen, why have you denied me?' She'd had no regular church background, but as a young girl had attended a Sunday School for just a few weeks where, for an exam, they had studied the life of Peter, the disciple who denied Jesus. But this was a test she had not been prepared for. This was God speaking. 'What is wrong with me? What is wrong with trusting Jesus?' she reasoned with herself, driving home late that night.

Only weeks later, Gwen knelt down, repented of her sin and knew in an instant that the One her husband had come to know, love and serve had become her Saviour and Lord. The Hound of Heaven had been silently at work 'with unhurrying chase, and unperturbed pace ...' patiently pursuing, lovingly convicting, powerfully saving another precious soul. Who can tell how many individuals were involved in the pursuit of Gwen through the years? But human instrumentality was inevitably required. Willing men and women who dared to be faithful witnesses for Christ, simply links in a chain.

Just a link

It is helpful seeing salvation as a chain of events. Although each person has the origins of their salvation in eternity past, it is worked out in time through a series of God-ordained events— precious links in God's priceless 'salvation chain'. No conversion, no matter how sudden or dramatic we consider the moment of new life to be, is without the links—that is, gracious, personal interventions of God, where He speaks a word or uses an incident in a person's life in preparation for the day of days when 'all heaven rejoices' as one more sinner is welcomed home.

When it comes to opportunities to share our faith, we must be sensitive to the promptings of the Holy Spirit to know when we have played our part, being freed from the pressure to 'get the whole gospel out' in one indigestible chunk. If we truly believe that salvation is God's work, we can be assured that if we are not in regular contact with the person concerned, then He will send another witness at just the right time for the next link or stage of his or her salvation.

This conviction, however, is not to provide us with an excuse to keep silent when we should speak, but to prevent us from being in panic mode, thinking all depends upon a faultless text book kind of performance. I remember hearing Rico Tice (Associate Minister of All Souls and author of

Christianity Explored) saying, 'People often ask me after a mission, "Rico, were many saved?" It's the wrong question. They should have asked me, "Rico, did you faithfully preach the gospel?"'

We need exactly the same mentality in one-on-one situations and should ask ourselves, 'Did I faithfully play my part/add the link required of me in that situation?' Naturally, we all would like to be the final link in leading someone to Christ, but if the person is not yet ready we can trust God to provide the next link at just the right time.

Tracts

The salvation link used by the Holy Spirit in so many conversions has been a Christian leaflet ('tracts' as we call them in the trade). Roger Carswell, the writer of dozens and distributor of thousands of tracts, says, 'I do not know of an easier way to share the good news of Jesus Christ than through a short, simple leaflet which fits into my wallet, pocket or bag and is an abiding message ready to go to work and be used by God at any time.'[16]

Gwen received a phone call one morning from a man with a very broad Scottish accent. She promptly passed the phone to me! He explained how he lived in a rural area in Aberdeenshire and had been visiting London a few weeks previously. Whilst walking through Covent Garden, he had been handed a leaflet, given by one of our Saturday outreach team. He then informed me earnestly, 'This message won't let me go!' We excitedly sensed that he was being 'pursued' and sent him a little pack of helpful booklets. We rejoiced when he phoned again shortly after to inform us that he had surrendered his life to Christ.

A year passed and we eagerly awaited news from north of the border, but all was quiet. He had previously told us that he had started attending a church to which he had to travel twenty-seven miles—the nearest evangelical church. So, with our typically pathetic faith, we presumed the worst, thinking that the seed had most probably been 'scorched' or 'choked' to death (Mark 4:6–7). However, a year later he telephoned to inform us that he had seen some of his family saved, had married a fine Christian woman, been on a mercy trip to Romania and, being burdened for his own area, had been instrumental in planting a church there and had already seen some conversions.

We were amazed, not only by what God had done in just one year but by how kind it was of Him to allow us to know these things for our encouragement. Of course, eternity alone will reveal the full extent of our labours for him, but we were shown just something of how God had been at work—and all could be traced back to one person handing a leaflet to a stranger. There is no telling what God can do if we have the humility and willingness to simply be a 'link'.

Prayer

Jim Elliot yearned to be a 'crisis man'—and there is nothing like a crisis to make us pray. Really pray! If we could but comprehend something of the 'lost-ness of the lost' we would all become crisis men and women, living lives of holy recklessness and this, out of necessity, would drive us to our knees. President J.F. Kennedy once remarked that 'When written in Chinese, the word "crisis" is composed of two characters; one represents danger, and the other represents opportunity.'

Every crisis provides us with an opportunity to trust God and cry out to Him for divine intervention. Warren Wiersbe challenges us to recognise the seriousness of the hour by directing us to the early church when, in their vulnerability and feeling of helplessness, the Christians cried out to God. 'Peter and John had just come in "from the trenches", and the church met to pray in order to defeat the enemy.

Too often today, believers gather for prayer as though attending a concert or a party. There's little sense of urgency or danger because most of us are comfortable in our Christian walk. If more of God's people were witnessing for Christ in daily life, there would be more urgency and blessing when the church meets for prayer.'[17]

Prayer is a ministry every Christian is called to exercise. There is little earthly glory in this particular branch of service, which is perhaps the reason why so few seek this ministry in the church. But how vital these pray-ers are in gospel work! I'm convinced eternity will reveal just how important those unsung heroes were in advancing the kingdom. Seth Joshua, the evangelist beautifully captured in Geraint Fielder's *Grace, Grit and Gumption*, was one of the central players in the spiritual awakening that preceded the Welsh 1904-05 revival. His appeal for more prayer for evangelistic activities provides us with insight into the mindset of those God was pleased to use to revive His work: 'Make the valley full of ditches. There are plenty of surface workers in the religious world. What we want are diggers, those who prepare reservoirs for the living water.'[18]

We come back again to the connection between evangelism and revival. But let us not think that revival is the end to all our problems. As spiritual activity is heightened, opposition becomes more intense. But the blessing is normally found in the midst of the battle. When we 'stick our necks out' for Christ, when we become risk-takers, deliberately placing ourselves in a position of vulnerability, it is then we can expect the Holy Spirit to equip us in measures beyond the norm.

Luke records in Acts 12 the account of Peter's dramatic angelic deliverance from prison. Yet it is also a comical picture of how God answers prayer even when faith is weak (verses 13–16). The answer to earnest prayer (Peter) is standing right outside the door, but the unbelieving believers don't have enough faith to let him in! This remarkable deliverance is a reminder of the awesome potential of prayer. 'It was the angel brought Peter out of prison, but was prayer brought the angel!' commented Puritan Thomas Watson.

Don't be put off, thinking you need to be among the 'super-saints'. Prayer rarely feels 'powerful' when we are engaged in it. Although there may be those precious times of liberty in prayer, it mostly seems just 'ordinary'. But prayer honours God and God honours prayer. When we pray, we are saying, 'God I believe in you.' So, just take the Lord at His word and pray! 'Ask and it will be given to you; seek and you will find; knock and the door will be opened to you. For everyone who asks receives; the one who seeks finds; and to the one who knocks, the door will be opened.' (Matthew 7:7–8). Don't wait until you feel like praying—just pray! One old prayer warrior, Moody Stuart, gave this advice: '1. Pray until you pray. 2. Pray until you are conscious of being heard. 3. Pray until you receive an answer.'[19]

Praying mums

I don't know how many 'prodigals' I have met over the years, particularly during night time outreaches on the streets and perhaps especially during my Leicester Square nights. Each

Thursday night I would join up with a team from the London City Mission, headed up by a wonderfully committed, highly organised, disciplined (and unashamedly dogmatic!) German LCM evangelist, Bernhard Wolfell.

Night time in Leicester Square would be dense, with people seeking a good time, and I regularly would have conversations with young people in whom I detected a certain 'something'—an openness to discuss spiritual things, a trace of guilt, an evident restraint and check upon their attempts to stray. Above all else, I received a sense that someone was praying for this young man or woman. Usually, when the young person was pressed, it would emerge that there was a praying mum somewhere in the background.

I believe there is a special power in the prayers of an anxious mother. I recently received, in the same week, two emails from two different mums, both of whom were unknown to me and to each other, relating completely differing circumstances in very different parts of the country. But they had one thing in common: they were mums who had young prodigals and I noticed that both used the same words in their request for prayer for their straying boys: 'I am desperate'.

I can't believe pleadings that are wrung from such anguished hearts will go unanswered by so gracious a God, who delights in both seeking prodigals and in healing the broken-hearted. I now have a category in my prayer diary: 'Desperate Mums'. We need to join with them in their travail and rejoice with them when the Hound of Heaven has tracked the wanderers down and brought them safely home.

Praying wives

Betty was a gracious, faithful Christian, married to Dilwyn, who was a good man, a paramedic, yet humanistic and atheistic in his outlook. He 'did his bit' for society and was 'pleased for Betty' that 'her religion did her good'. When I visited the home, Dil would usher me into the lounge and then politely leave me to do the 'religious bit' whilst he moved on to more practical manly matters. One couldn't help feeling wimpish as Dil, a broad-shouldered six-footer, left the room.

However, I began to discern a gradual change in him after he was diagnosed with a life-threatening illness. This keen gardener would linger when I visited and make some comment on how there must be 'someone behind the scenes' who gives life, makes things grow, etc. As time passed, Dil would hover around and then stay in the room as I read the Scriptures and prayed with Betty.

We invited them both to our home for dinner and a friendship developed, albeit a short one, as not long after he was taken into hospital a very ill man. Even then, I did not expect Betty's call that was to bring the good news. 'Hello Pastor!' chirped the excited Welsh valleys voice on the telephone, 'Dil has come through!' My mind, being elsewhere, in the middle of sermon preparation, thought, 'Come through what?' 'He has trusted the Lord', Betty qualified. I expressed how pleased I was and yet, putting the phone down, I was still inwardly grappling with how God could be so gracious to someone who had not yet come to church on a Sunday! But 'come through' Dil most certainly had, as for his remaining weeks on earth he showed a genuine love and gratitude towards the One who had loved him and given His life for him. One factor that cannot be left out, however, is that

Betty had prayed for her stubborn husband for over forty years!

Praying friends and work colleagues

Whilst my personal life was rapidly spiralling downwards through drink, unknown to me the young man who had been witnessing to me had taken the situation to his church youth group for prayer. All these young people knew was that there was a 'hopeless case' named Mike in need of Jesus. But we have a God 'who is able to do immeasurably more than all we ask or imagine', who not only wonderfully answered prayer to save, but called both men to be preachers of this mighty Saviour and who were ordained as Baptist ministers together on the same day. The young man who so faithfully and courageously shared his faith, Paul Pease, is now pastor of Hook Evangelical Church in Surbiton. I will be eternally grateful to God for him—and to those 'behind the scenes' who prayed.

Praying sons

My mother was a comical, yet at times acerbic, Liverpudlian ('I'm not a sinner son, I'm from Liverpoooool!'). She took no prisoners! In fairness, my father, who was a professional musician, had not given her the easiest of lives. But the Lord saved her uniquely, as He does each of us, and the final link in her chain of salvation was a letter!

Two years after my conversion we moved away from Bournemouth as a family for my studies at a Bible College in South Wales and I felt an increasing burden for my mother who was not in good health. I was deeply concerned that by our moving out of the area the chances of her being saved were gone. One night I had an awful dream in which she had died. I stood in the funeral home gazing at her frail, lifeless frame in her coffin. When I awoke, her eternal lostness hit me hard and I felt the Holy Spirit stirring me to write to her. It was a short, simple, heart-felt letter. 'Dear Mum, I'm writing to say how much I love you, and that without Jesus saving you, nothing will stop you going to hell when you die.'

It would have won no literary prize. But, boy, didn't God graciously attach to it a Holy Spirit eloquence! On receiving it, my mother was taken straight to her knees where she repented of her sin and asked the Lord to save her. She phoned excitedly to tell me. Her voice was different. She spoke of feeling so clean and happy. But the real test that would alone convince me that she had been genuinely converted was to meet her.

We visited her some weeks later and, besides her looking so different, she stunned us by apologising to Gwen, asking her forgiveness for the way she had treated her so harshly in the past. My mum didn't do apologies! Well, we rejoiced together and I was reminded so clearly that 'salvation comes from the Lord' (Jonah 2:9). It is He who pursues and renews. But we must pray.

4 The Ministry of the Spirit

Thank God for the work of the Holy Spirit, guiding, prodding, leading, scattering, cajoling and herding us into our God-given opportunities

William Wade[20]

We are privileged to live in post-Pentecost days, when the Holy Spirit is now poured out on all people (Acts 2:17) in order that the good news of Jesus Christ may be taken to all the world. But God has always been the 'missionary God' and as we read the Old Testament it is thrilling to see His plan of redemption unfolding. Abraham will be 'the father of many nations' (Genesis 17:4) and the covenant with Israel given to Moses would give way to a new covenant.

Paul, writing to the church in first century pagan Corinth, wants them to grasp the wonder of this. Speaking of the lesser and the greater glory, he reasons, 'Now if the ministry that brought death, which was engraved in letters on stone, came with glory, so that the Israelites could not look steadily at the face of Moses because of its glory, transitory though it was, will not the ministry of the Spirit be even more glorious? If the ministry that brought condemnation was glorious, how much more glorious is the ministry that brings righteousness!' (2 Corinthians 3:7–9).

Paul sounds almost breathless in seeking to get his hearers to grasp the wonder of it all. Not spiritual death, but life! Not condemnation, but righteousness! Not a fading glory, but an ever increasing one! As twenty-first century believers, one of the greatest dangers we face is being heart-dead to the immeasurable privilege of being New Covenant believers, indwelt personally by the Spirit of the living God. The veil has been removed and we enjoy a life of freedom, free to live and to love as God intended. We are not those who are simply 'doing our duty' but, rather, are now filled and motivated by divine love. Duty, of course has its place, but as Phillips Brooks says, 'Duty makes us do things well, but love makes us do them beautifully.'[21]

The Holy Spirit in the Old Testament

Let us be careful, however, not to overlook the importance of the ministry of the Spirit in the Old Testament, because God's people have always had to look to Him for His power. Although there is no record of the Spirit dwelling within people, as we now enjoy, we do read of Him coming upon judges, kings, prophets, priests, the inspired psalmists, as well as seeing Him give gifts to equip craftsmen for their specialist work. We notice Him coming powerfully upon particular people, at particular times, for particular purposes. Being led and guided by God is, of course, not restricted to evangelistic endeavours and throughout the Scriptures we see God's people being directed in all kinds of situations and circumstances. We see this, for example, in the lives of Abraham and David.

Abraham seeks a wife for his precious son Isaac, but is aware that he has no cast-iron guarantee of success. He says to his servant, 'If the woman is unwilling to come back with you, then you will be released from this oath of mine.' (Genesis 24:8). But he did send him forth with a measure of faith and expectancy, believing that it was the will of God for Isaac to shun taking a wife from the daughters of the Canaanites. And then we observe the heart-warming faith and concern of the servant: '... he prayed, "LORD, God of my master Abraham, make me successful today, and show kindness to my master Abraham"' (24:12).

It is a beautiful love story with a happy ending. After travelling for a month, the servant arrives at just the right place, meets just the right girl, at just the right time and receives just the right response from her and her family. When safely home with his catch, his heart bursts with thankfulness at the thrill of being so led and used by God and he testifies how '... I bowed down and worshipped the Lord. I praised the Lord, the God of my master Abraham, who had led me on the right road to get the granddaughter of my master's brother for his son' (24:48).

David was 'a man after God's own heart'. God testified concerning him: 'I have found David son of Jesse a man after my own heart; he will do everything I want him to do' (Acts 13:22). We might well ask why, with all the evident flaws in his life, although unquestionably a great king and leader, was David singled out in such a way?

His chequered life is a record of phenomenal success and abysmal failure, but the reason he towered above all others was that his ear was ever inclined toward God, seeking to be an instrument in His hands. His greatest fear is crystal clear in his penitential Psalm 51: 'Do not cast me from your presence or take your Holy Spirit from me. Restore to me the joy of your salvation ... THEN I will teach transgressors your ways, so that sinners will turn back to you.' (51:11–13. Whether fighting lions, bears, giants or inner battles with his own sinful nature, this passionate man sought to 'keep in step with Spirit'.

Clay pots

No doubt the reason why God has been able to use men and women throughout the millennia, despite their obvious flaws, is that they burnt with the same fiery desires as David. One of the great encouragements I receive from Christian biography (if the biographer is honest enough to include the 'warts and all' in the life of his subject) is to notice that the greatest of our heroes throughout the history of the church have all had their flaws, failings and foibles—without exception.

Whether the domestically disastrous John Wesley, the over-authoritarian William Booth or the oft times reckless C.T. Studd, they all had a single eye to pleasing God and set the world alight whilst others fumbled with the box of matches. We saw earlier how the character of the messenger matters and for this reason we dare not be lacking in the area of discernment regarding gospel work and workers. Yet we can expend much time and energy examining the personality or theology of men and women, searching for reasons why God should not use them and be in danger of writing off those whom He can use despite their imperfections.

In the final analysis, we are all pretty ropey material in the service of the King or, as the Apostle Paul puts it, 'we have this treasure in jars of clay' and because of the weakness of the vessel it goes to prove that the 'all surpassing power is from God and not from us' (2 Corinthians 4:7). For this reason we need to be slow to criticise.

Dwight L. Moody, the former shoe salesman whom God mightily used internationally as an evangelist, was once criticised for the methods he practised. A lady remarked, 'Mr. Moody, I don't like the way you do evangelism!' 'Well, ma'am, let me ask you, how do you do it', Moody asked. She replied, 'I don't!' Moody responded, 'Well, I like my way of doing it better than your way of not doing it!' We really do need to beware of harbouring a critical Spirit-quenching attitude, but rather to actually pray for gospel success for those not of our tribe.

The great Apostle Paul is in prison, shut out of the action, when he is given reports of certain preachers who 'preach Christ out of envy and rivalry ... out of selfish ambition, not sincerely' seeking to stir up trouble for him. What is his response? 'What does it matter? The important thing is that in every way, whether from false motives or true, Christ is preached. And because of this I rejoice.' (Philippians 1:15, 17–18). Oh, for such large-hearted, self-abasing leaders! Let us be encouraged by the fact that our gracious God is continuously looking for those whose eyes are fixed on Him, waiting in total dependence for daily guidance into situations of usefulness and witness. 'For the eyes of the LORD range throughout the earth to strengthen those whose hearts are fully committed to him.' (2 Chronicles 16:9).

Seeking to be Spirit-led

'I only evangelise when I get a fuzzy feeling', a sincere young guy shared with one of our street outreach teams one day. My personal reaction to such a view is that if that were the case, I would hardly ever venture outside the front door to attempt anything for Jesus! There is always the danger that, in seeking to be sensitive to the guidance of the Holy Spirit, we become a slave to our feelings. Seeking to 'keep in step with the Spirit' (to use J. I. Packer's phrase) should never prevent us taking and making opportunities to share the gospel, at any time and in any place. In his Journals, John Wesley, undoubtedly one of the world's most successful evangelists, shares a humorous account of an experiment he once tried.

For these two days I had made an experiment which I had been so often and earnestly pressed to do—speaking to none concerning the things of God unless my heart was free to it. And what was the event? Why, 1. That I spoke to none at all for fourscore miles together; no, not even to him that traveled with me in the chaise, unless a few words at first setting out; 2. That I had no cross either to bear or to take up, and commonly, in an hour or two, fell fast asleep; 3. That I had much respect shown me wherever I came, everyone behaving to me as to a civil, good-natured gentleman. Oh, how pleasing is all this to flesh and blood![22]

This lesson, which Wesley learned by his experiment, is of vital importance; we must be convinced that it is our responsibility as Christians to share the gospel with anyone and everyone and at any time but, of course, 'with gentleness and respect' (1 Peter 3:15). John Stott's book, *Our Guilty Silence*, was written out of concern that the church had not been as faithful in spreading the gospel as she ought. His words are strong and make us uncomfortable: 'Our silence has condemned men to death and misery and darkness', he says. We must speak. But sensitivity to the Holy Spirit's leading in our witness should be a priority when seeking seeking guidance. Do I just chat about general matters or move into the spiritual at present? What is the best way into the gospel with this person? How far do I go? How long shall I speak? etc.

We dare not doubt God's willingness to direct us and we are to live in the daily expectation of seeking to be led by the Spirit into a life of holy obedience to God's will, doing what He wants us to do in the place where He wants us to be. Not for one minute must we think that being in the centre of God's will and being led by the Spirit means we will be cocooned from discomfort or embarrassment! Anglican minister and author Michael Green pointedly reminds us of the outgoing and disturbing nature of the Holy Spirit: 'The Comforter does not come to make believers comfortable, but to make them missionaries.'[23]

We must not shrink back in fear, but push forward, trusting the Holy Spirit to give us the boldness we need for the job. George Verwer, the founder of Operation Mobilisation, says forthrightly, 'Without Holy Spirit boldness, the world will remain unevangelized... there can never be a substitute for the power of the Spirit working through willing men and women, and that power will bring boldness.'

Out of our comfort zone

Seeking to be led and used by the Spirit, I believe, is to enjoy the drama of expecting the unexpected, being prepared to find ourselves in situations that take us beyond our natural abilities and being cast entirely upon the power and wisdom of God. Some years ago I was led into a situation, the significance of which beforehand I failed to recognise; it took me way outside my comfort zone. If we accept one definition of this oft used phrase as 'a situation where one feels safe or at ease', then I was certainly outside of it.

At the time we were involved in a work in Central London and I, together with Gwen and our two youngest daughters, Victoria and Rebecca, was living in the heart of the bustling and perhaps bizarre area of Covent Garden. As a resident and local minister, I was invited by the local Community Association to attend a hearing in the City of Westminster Magistrates Court to support those seeking to oppose a local nightclub owner, a high profile, ageing, outlandish, but charismatic, playboy/entrepreneur/celebrity. His latest venture was to apply for a licence that would allow lap-dancing in his club, which being the first of its kind in the

West End meant this would be a landmark case. I reluctantly agreed to attend and as I walked sluggishly from my home through Trafalgar Square, Parliament Square and into the Horseferry Road Court, I inwardly grumbled all the way, thinking of all the important stuff I needed to do.

In the tense, packed courtroom, the applicant wasn't hard to miss, with his flowing blond locks and surrounded by close friends and colleagues. He had hired a bright, attractive, eloquent female barrister to represent him and, to this day, I am astounded as to how anything so sordid could be described in such an everyday, harmless, sanitised way. But this was a wealthy man and able to afford the best legal team. Various residents gave reasons why the licence should not be granted. The magistrate then put to all in court, 'Is there anyone here who would like to cross-examine Mr. S?'

Silence. But then (the only way I can explain it is feeling as though I was being picked up by the back of my jacket) I found myself on my feet! I vividly remember the feeling of sheer panic as all eyes locked on me. But then they came—one, two, three, four questions fired one after the other. So amazed was I, that I wrote them down afterwards:

> Is Mr. S. aware of the harm that can follow from this kind of club? (I expanded on this a little.)

> Is Mr. S. aware that despite the lovely packaging of this club, it is sheer titillation, isn't it? (I went on to expound on this a little also, explaining that we all have a dark side to our nature that needs no encouraging.)

Here, the defendant didn't attempt an answer but, evidently flustered, interjected 'Let's lighten things up a little!'

> Mr. S., why this new departure in the kind of club you run?

> Mr. S,. what are your motives? Personal? Financial?

I can only compare the experience to the liberty given by the Holy Spirit on occasions in the act of preaching and I'm unable to describe the immense love, compassion and pity that filled my heart for Mr. S. and the group with him. I sat down and there was a break in the proceedings. Mr. S. immediately approached me, extremely pleasant and charming. In fact over the next few days he would walk over to chat with me in court. Although I was suspicious of his motives, my encouragement was that I felt this was a man with a conscience that was alive, but there was a battle raging.

On the final day, in the break before the decision was announced, he said, 'Mike, you know, if I fail this time, I will only apply again'. I felt I was given a verse of Scripture for him. 'Peter, the Scripture says, "Even in laughter the heart may ache" (Proverbs 14:13).'

Needless to say, the moral case carries no weight these days and the licence was granted. Providentially, we met on a number of occasions over the years and chatted, once whilst I was preaching in Covent Garden Market, and each time we parted I sensed that here was a man who was being given opportunities to 'seek the LORD while he may be found; call on him while he is near' and to hear the plea for 'the wicked [to] forsake their ways' (Isaiah 55:6–7).

I remain personally convinced that there was more to our meetings than met the eye and that this was yet another being pursued by the gracious Hound of Heaven. Did he attend Sunday School as a working class lad in Yorkshire? Had he had contact with other Christians through the years? I just sensed there was a wrestling, a tugging at his soul. We will look later at what it is to 'resist the Holy Spirit'.24

5 The Spirit and The Word

All Scripture is God-breathed (2 Timothy 3:16)

The Bible is none other than the voice of him that sitteth upon the throne. Every book of it, every chapter of it, every syllable of it, every letter of it. It is the direct utterance of the Most High.

John William Burgon[25]

We have monumental truths to impart—truths that are indispensable and vital for each and every living person, yet are considered totally outrageous to the typical twenty-first century Westerner. We have the audacity to speak with authority on subjects like heaven, hell, life, death, sexuality, judgement and much more. When we share our faith, the response more often than not will be, 'Well, who do you think you are?' 'Who gives you the authority to say these things?'

This is where the rubber hits the road. As hard as it might be for people living in a society that knows nothing but relativism, we have no alternative but to bite the bullet and inform them, 'All that I am telling you comes from the Bible.' We minister in a society that declares (absolutely), 'There is no such thing as absolute truth!' Their belief system is, 'Believe whatever you want. Do whatever seems best to you. Live for whatever brings you pleasure, as long as it doesn't hurt anyone.' And, of course, 'Be tolerant. Don't tell anyone that their beliefs are wrong.' (Unless, of course, they are Bible-believing Christians.)

Not our battle

As intimidated or embarrassed as we may feel at times, it is a tremendous burden lifted when we are able to rest the complete weight of what we are seeking to share upon the shoulders of the eternal Word of God. As a brand new believer, I was able to tell those around that I had become a follower of Jesus Christ. I was able to explain very little about the faith I had entered, but found enormous comfort from a plaque which I placed on my wall, which proclaimed authoritatively: 'Your word, Lord, is eternal; it stands firm in the heavens' (Psalm 119:89).

It provides endless comfort to know that 'the battle is not yours, but God's' (2 Chronicles 20:15) and so you can trust Him for the outcome following the truths you graciously seek to share, no matter if these are met with rolling eyes, pitying sighs or irate cries.

Spirit of truth

Our Saviour, preparing His disciples for their task—which is now ours—was only too aware of the resistance the gospel would meet and therefore encouraged them by speaking of the One coming after Him: 'the Spirit of truth. The world cannot accept him, because it neither sees him nor knows him. But you know him, for he lives with you and will be in you.' (John 14:17). How reassuring is that?! The Holy Spirit who is the author of all Scripture lives within you! The Holy Spirit who has been sent to 'prove the world to be in the wrong about sin and righteousness and judgment' (John 16:8) is for you!

It is our job simply to be channels, 'instruments... useful to the Master and prepared to do any good work.' (2 Timothy 2:21). It is the Holy Spirit alone who can change a person so that, when they too are converted and indwelt by the divine Author, they will then know that Jesus is Lord and that the gospel is true. Whenever the Holy Spirit breathes spiritual life into a man or woman, boy or girl, He breathes into them a love, desire and need for His Word. The book that previously was locked, dull and irrelevant is now suddenly open, alive and as vital as food and drink.

Confidence

If you are put on the spot and the question is fired at you, 'Why do you believe the Bible is the Word of God?' it is good to have a good, short, confident reply. Here is a useful five-pointer (of course, you can expound the points if you able):

1.   Our need of revelation.
2.   The amazing unity and harmony of the Bible. (Written over a period of 1500 years, by over 40 authors.)
3.   The fulfilled prophecies.
4.   Its preservation, despite constant attack. (Still the world's best seller!)
5.   Its life-changing power.

Relevance

If asked about the relevance of this 'old book' for today, you could testify (using Steve Levy's words):

It makes me understand myself.
It makes me understand the world.
It is my light, my life, my hope, my guide, my joy.
It show me how to clean up the mess I make of my life at times.
It gives advice in all circumstances.

It gives me strength when I feel weak.

It gives comfort.

It makes sense of my suffering.

It gives purpose to my existence.

It saves my life.

It makes me wise.

It saves me from my enemies.

It makes me cry, and is my delight.

It makes me solid as a Christian.

It teaches me to praise.[26]

The Holy Spirit exalts the written Word

It is a fact seen in Scripture and throughout Church history that, whenever there has been a significant work of the Holy Spirit, the Word of God is always exalted and becomes pre-eminent. Nehemiah was instrumental in re-building the city wall, but much more was going on as God used him to bring revival to His people. It is significant that when the Spirit stirs the people, they spontaneously gather together to seek God and to hear His voice. Eternal things now take priority and they command Ezra the scribe to 'bring out the Book ...' (Nehemiah 8:1). Ezra proceeds to read it aloud from daybreak till noon to men, women and children. (8: 2–3). There is weeping and rejoicing. God is at work! But note, the Spirit of God is exalting the Word of God. This is always the case, simply because the written Word speaks, cover to cover of Christ, the living Word, who is in 'all the Scriptures' (Luke 24:27).

From Genesis to Revelation, the Bible reveals how God saves sinners through His one and only Son, the Lord Jesus Christ. Christ is the heart of the Scriptures, the heart of history, the heart of the universe and it is the work of the

Holy Spirit to reveal this wonderful reality to spiritually hungry men and women of every generation.

Reformation and revival

It is the sixteenth century and deep darkness covers Europe. But the Holy Spirit stirs and light breaks out from various sources. Martin Luther in Germany is a key player, of course. We then see William Tyndale, a private tutor to a family in Gloucester, with a growing burden. Armed with his little Greek New Testament, and deeply exercised by the Holy Spirit, he disputes with high ranking deans, abbots and bishops, exclaiming boldly, 'God helping me I will cause the boy that drives the plough to know more of the Scriptures than thou dost!' Hunted, imprisoned and eventually sentenced to death, he cries out just before being burnt, 'Lord, open the King of England's eyes!' Two years later, his dying prayer is answered and a copy of the Scriptures is placed in every parish church in England.

The Spirit of God exalts the Word of God. It was, and always is, so. If you read any history on revival, you will see that chief among the various fruits following a move of the Spirit is a greater love, respect, and honouring of the Bible and an increased dependency on it. There is ever the temptation to separate the Spirit from the Word, but the great need in every generation is for Spirit-anointed preaching of the Word of God. Extremes will cause us either to wither and have low expectancy or to wander and embrace a fantasy faith.

Michael Reeves and Tim Chester provide a timely reminder as to *Why the Reformation Still Matters* in their vibrant book of that title. They state that the Reformers made much about hearing God's voice through the Scriptures in the power of the Spirit, teaching that, 'We not only hear God's voice in his Word; we experience his presence'. Then, continuing on the theme of the relevance of their doctrine in our day, they say, 'This is precisely why the Reformers' theology of the Spirit is so necessary for the church's health today; it means the difference between that zombie religiosity the West has grown so sick of and a living faith that can transform it ... we so need the Reformers' theology of the Spirit to help preserve us from such empty formalism.'[27]

A dying world needs a living church. It is, then, our duty to love, guard, cherish, use and have utter confidence in the Scriptures at all times, whether they are prized, pilloried or simply passed over in the days in which we live. Times may change but, we can be sure, the Spirit will always honour the Word.

Eternity and the Word

The greater our sense of eternity, the greater we shall treasure and depend upon the Scriptures. Listen to John Wesley's testimony:

> To candid, reasonable men, I am not afraid to lay open what have been the inmost thoughts of my heart. I have thought, I am a creature of a day, passing through life as an arrow through the air. I am a spirit come from God, and returning to God: just hovering over the great gulf; till, a few moments hence, I am no more seen; I drop into an unchangeable eternity! I want to know one thing,—the way to heaven; how to land safe on that happy shore. God himself has condescended to teach me the way. For this very end He came from heaven. He hath written it down in a book. O give me that book! At any price, give me the book of God![28]

Use the sword

The Psalmist wrote, 'The unfolding of your word gives light' (Psalm 119:130). Never lose confidence in the Word, 'For the word of God is alive and active. Sharper than any double-edged sword, it penetrates even to dividing soul and spirit, joints and marrow; it judges the thoughts and attitudes of the heart.' (Hebrews 4:12). Whether seeking to communicate God's Word as preachers, or sharing one-on-one, we mustn't be put off by any reaction, whether anger or indifference. The Spirit of God can take the Word of God and do things that neither we nor the person hearing may be aware of! 'The Spirit of God speaks through his Word in ways that can't be measured, explained or controlled. God's Spirit speaks through Scripture and gets into our bones and marrow and sinks into our consciousness in extraordinary ways', writes Rebecca Manley Pippert.[29]

The conscience, the 'ally' planted within the hearer, is able to take the things we have spoken and recall them to hearers weeks, months or even years later and at times and in situations they least expect. I have had people approach me on numerous occasions saying things like, 'I don't know if you remember me, but two years ago, you said ...' I had forgotten all about it, but their conscience hadn't!

It is a wonderful fact that you cannot unhear what you have heard. There have been occasions when the person with whom I am attempting to share the gospel has seemed utterly impervious, even dismissive, regarding my efforts: 'I am an atheist; this is entire rot!' (or words to that effect). But, mindful of my collaborator living within him, I say calmly and gently, with a genuinely warm smile, something like this, 'I know you don't believe this, but the Bible says, "people are destined to die once, and after that to face judgment."' (Hebrews 9:27).

On almost every occasion I have witnessed the Word of God having an effect. Either the conversation has suddenly sparked into life or there has been a humbling on the part of my atheist friend. But even if there is no reaction, I have planted truth into his mind. He will stand before his Maker one day.

Centre on the living Word

Paul Williams, in his book *Intentional*, quotes renowned Bible teacher John Stott: 'In evangelism ... our chief and overriding responsibility is to point people to Jesus ... the wisest evangelist keeps bringing the conversation back to the person and work of Jesus Christ.'[30] Christ is the heart of the gospel, the heart of the Scriptures, the heart of the universe. God is Spirit. He is unseen, but Christ is 'the image of the invisible God', the One sent into the world to reconcile us to God, 'by making peace through his blood, shed on the cross' (Colossians 1:15, 20).

It is the work of the Holy Spirit to glorify Christ by revealing Him to men and women. Jesus Himself said, 'He [the Holy Spirit] will glorify me because it is from me that he will receive what he will make known to you.' (John 16:14). The Holy Spirit never points to Himself, but always away, to Christ. J.I. Packer[31] says that just as a well-placed floodlight points away from itself to the chosen object, so the 'shy' Holy Spirit illumines Jesus. Just as the Holy Spirit exalts the written Word, He supremely exalts Christ, the living Word. If we desire to be used in our witnessing or preaching, we must focus on the person of Christ (God incarnate) and why He came (to die for sinners). Spurgeon said that we must always seek to 'make a bee-line to the cross'.

Sword of the Spirit

Having reminded ourselves 'the battle is God's', we must not be negligent and go into battle unequipped. Paul Williams challenges us: 'I always have a Bible with me. Even on the tennis court, in my tennis bag... years ago, someone said to me, "Never go without a Bible with you—it's the sword of the Spirit, and we're in battle. Why would you want to go anywhere without your sword?"'[32] In these technological days, where we have access to all kinds of electronic gadgetry, we have absolutely no excuse to be sword-less! It is clear to see that God has equipped us with all that we need for the task He has given us. The disturbing question is, 'Why are we so reluctant?'

6 Fire!

Truth must have an attendant fire that is alive and coming from the very presence of God

Zack Eswine[33]

I want you young men always to bear in mind that it is the nature of fire to go out; you must keep it stirred and fed, and the ashes removed.

William Booth, addressing a group of young Salvation Army officers[34]

Hell fire?

Why is it there is such a reluctance among us as Christians to speak about Christ? We are all fearful of the response we may get—in the West, little more serious than ridicule, rebuke or rejection. But I don't think for a moment that our foot-dragging is due to a lack of knowledge. Whilst we can always benefit from training, seminars and the like, surely the real problem is that of motivation or, rather, lack thereof.

Ironically, we evangelicals hold firm convictions regarding the fact that all are lost and heading for an eternity in hell without salvation through Jesus Christ. Yes, it is a pretty stark bottom line and the subject truly is awful to contemplate. We write articles and books, give papers to defend this essential biblical doctrine and would go to war against those who deny it—and rightly so. But somehow this solemn truth doesn't seem to reach our hearts and compel us to go out in rescue mode as it ought. If we are honest, we are embarrassed by the logic of C.T. Studd, who cried in exasperated disbelief,

'How can a man believe in Hell unless he throws away his life to rescue others from its torment?' If he is right in his reasoning, then surely our greatest need is not so much to have evangelism and mission on our church agendas but, rather, have the desire to somehow reach the unsaved multitudes burnt into our very hearts and souls.

We might feel a little more comfortable if able to write off Studd's words as those of an extremist: 'After all he was a little odd, wasn't he?' But the problem is, it is the truth that hits us, hurts us and haunts us. People really are lost without Jesus and we His followers have the sole charge of telling this to a perishing world. We therefore cannot see evangelism and mission as options some Christians or church members may show an interest in.

If the Holy Spirit is the Director of Evangelism and dwells in the heart of every child of God, then alarm bells should be ringing, warning that all is not well with us spiritually. We might well have good theological (and physiological!) reasons for criticising William Booth for saying, 'If I thought I could win one more soul to the Lord by walking on my head and playing the tambourine with my toes, I'd learn how'. But this, surely, is the language of holy desperation—words wrung from the heart of a man with convictions about the 'lost-ness' of men and women who were hell-bound without the Saviour who had loved and rescued him.

God a consuming fire

Our God is a consuming fire; He burns with holy love and holy anger. If this is true, then there should surely be something fire-like about those who claim to be indwelt by Him. Amy Carmichael, whose passionate love was poured out in India, rescuing little girls from a life of abuse, prayed for herself:

Give me the love that leads the way,
The faith that nothing can dismay,
The hope no disappointments tire,
The passion that will burn like fire;
Let me not sink to be a clod;
Make me Thy fuel, Flame of God

That beautiful word 'passion' has been hijacked, debased and used continually by anyone about anything. By cut-throat wannabees on *The Apprentice*, who would boil their grandmothers in oil for a lucrative job, TV 'personalities' boasting about their passion for food, sport, career, garden, wine, collections of moths, etc.

Webster's Dictionary defines passion as 'extreme, compelling emotion or intense emotional drive', but if our world really wants to know what passion means, then we are forced to look at Jesus Christ, at His intense love, selfless life, direst suffering, sacrificial death and glorious resurrection. He was stripped that we might be clothed, He died that we might live, was punished that we might be pardoned, bore God's holy wrath that we might know His holy love, was forsaken that we might be accepted, was treated as God's enemy that we might become His friends, was wounded that we might be healed, tormented that we might be comforted and endured our hell that we might enjoy His heaven. This, surely, is passion. But now our precious Saviour has gone back to heaven and it rests with us, His people, to somehow communicate His life and message by our words and actions. How utterly impossible! Unless the Spirit of Jesus lives within us!

Holy Spirit fire

None of us is up to the task and *fear* is number one on our list of reasons of why we shrink back from the work we have been given to do and sadly admit to the truth that the 'fear of man will prove to be a snare.' (Proverbs 29:25). However, we are not expected to go in our own strength, but to seek that 'power from on high'.

Joseph of Arimathea, we are told, was undoubtedly a follower of Christ, but 'secretly because he feared the Jewish leaders.' (John 19:38). No doubt he justified his cowardice, as we all tend to do. He was a wealthy, respected man in the community and to be known as a follower of the despised Jesus of Nazareth could mean the end of his career and influence. Shame upon shame, even though his Master had hung naked publicly on a cross of shame, bearing the wrath for his sins, he was more concerned about his own reputation. However, the day came when he 'came out' and, taking a bold step, went to the Roman Governor, Pilate, asking for the lifeless body of Jesus, to provide a tomb for Him. It was to be the glorious defining moment of his life. Could this be your problem? Do you need to take some daring step for Christ so you can be set free?

William Patteson Nicholson was a man who just under a century ago lit a flame of revival in Northern Ireland and thousands were brought into the kingdom through his ministry. He was undoubtedly a 'character' and known for his forthrightness, but perhaps not so well known was the inner battle he had in order to overcome his reluctance to surrender the loss of his reputation in the eyes of the world. In a humorous biographical thumbnail sketch of the man, the unique Ulster preacher, pastor and politician Rev. Ian Paisley allows Nicholson himself to recall how he 'caught the fire' and was transformed. Try and 'hear' with a thick Belfast accent!:

> Friend, you will not think me egotistical if I put a wee bit
> of testimony in? I was willing to have done with
> everything under God's heaven but my reputation. I

tried to enter into a covenant with God that He would respect me as a Presbyterian. (We stand for dignity and decorum). I said, 'Lord, if I have to shout and if I have to make a fool of myself, and if I have—Oh, no, Lord, anything but that, anything but that.'

We have been Presbyterians since ever they came out of the ark, have always been, and it is ingrained in me. You think the way I behave sometimes is as if I did not know how to behave. If you only knew what it costs me to do the other! But it was the thing God put His hand on. 'Go down on Saturday night to Main Street in Bangor, North of Ireland and give your testimony in the Salvation Army.' 'On Saturday night? Lord, I will go to China ...' 'No you will not; you will go down to Main Street.' 'Lord, I will do—' 'No you will confess Me.' ... 'Lord, I will give up all my money.' 'No, go down there and make a fool of yourself.'

Thirty-five years ago the Salvation Army was not respectable like it is now; you lost everything when you joined that bunch—but you got everything that God had to give you. And our Salvation Army was two girls and a daft fool; there was not another creature. Daft Jimmy carried the flag, two wee lieutenants did the rest. If the Lord had said, 'On a Monday night', I would not have minded, there were not many people in, but everybody comes in from the country on Saturday night.

For three months I fought God on that thing, and so desperate did I become on Saturday afternoon coming down from business in the Bangor, County Down, railway train, there was nobody in the carriage and I got down on my knees and fervently and believingly prayed God to wreck the train and break my neck and take me to heaven. When I got home my mother said, 'You are not looking very well.' 'Well?' I says, 'I am dying.' 'You

73

had better take your dinner.' 'It would choke me.' I went to my room and locked the door, and I will not tell you how I talked to God or you would be shocked. In the heat of my spirit I told God a few things, but He didn't bother His head about that; He had been used to dealing with Irish. There is a lot of humour in God, that is why He loves the Irish so much, and why He made so many of them.

God you are going through with this blessing, make up your mind you will go through and, if you take my advice, do not tell Him what you will not do. Well, I got down there and I kept gazing in a shop window and back at those two. Oh, what I endured! The pains of hell were nothing and at last I turned round and stood on the kerb looking at those two and the fool, and every now and then there would be a clap on the back, and 'Hullo, there, Willie!' Says I, 'I have to go through; I have gone this far, I may as well go.' I stepped into that ring, two women and a fool, and that wee girl. She said, 'These people don't want to hear what we are saying, let us go down on our knees and pray for them.'

Two women and a fool and a Presbyterian down on their knees! Well, I could not stand; I had to get down; and there were the gutters—market gutters and it had been raining, and on my knees! I was wishing she would pray as long as the 119th Psalm, but in those days a Salvation Army prayer was like a telegram. She opened her eyes and the crowd was all around and I got up with the gutters running down my shins and I stood, hot with indignation. You could have boiled a kettle with what was coming off me, and I kept my head down and listened to the laughing of those relatives mocking and jeering at me. And she nudged me and said, 'The lieutenant will sing and you will take up the collection.' And they began throwing in the money—pennies, ha'pennies and sixpences. They said, 'Man, this is great.' And I was standing there, in my heart mad as a hatter. After she got her collection she said, 'We are going round to the Barracks. Brother, you take the tambourine and lead us down the street.'

Well, I was enough Irish not to let a woman beat me. Whenever I had put my hand on that tambourine something happened. I went up in the air with a shout and a whoop and the joy of the Lord hit me and the bottom went out of the tambourine and I went down that street with old Jimmy after me, and up to 2 o'clock on Sunday morning we had a great time. I lost something that day I never want to get back and I got something I never want to lose.[35]

That day, Nicholson lost his reputation—but he gained the fire! Let me ask, is there something *you* need to do, like Joseph of Arimathea, like W. P. Nicholson? Could the Holy Spirit be prompting you to take a plucky step in order to set you free from the snare, bringing you into a new place of liberty and usefulness?

The Love of God poured out into our hearts

Could the problem be that we are too dependent on our own puny resources to overcome fear, indifference or cowardice? We dare never lose sight of the supernatural dimension to the Christian faith. The Holy Spirit is the glorious link between the seeking infinite Creator of the universe and the fleeing, finite, earth-bound sinner. It is He who lovingly pursued you and convicted you of sin. It is He who first breathed new life into you and gave you heavenly desires. Christians are people who rest and rejoice in the finished work of Jesus Christ accomplished for them over two thousand years ago. Your peace and joy, therefore, flow not from anything you could ever do for God, but entirely from what He has done for you in the life, death and resurrection of His Son.

Speaking of the fruit of justification by faith, Paul states that, 'God's love has been poured out into our hearts through the Holy Spirit, who has been given to us' (Romans 5:5). Robert Horn said, 'God's love is always supernatural, always a miracle, always the last thing we deserve.'[36] The Spirit comes loaded with God's love, with the aim of filling our little earthly frames with heavenly glory. Can this possibly happen without our being aware of it?

I am convinced that the greater our assurance of God's love for us, the more likely we are to speak of Him to others. Even though we be in the midst of trial, rejection or suffering, it this love which enables us to be 'more than conquerors' (Romans 8:37) as we take Christ to a hard, hostile world. If this experience seems foreign to us, then we must earnestly seek God for this, our 'birthright', so that our hearts can then respond with the cry Abba, Father' (Romans 8:15). Yet, the fact remains that no matter how earth-shatteringly powerful an experience of the Holy Spirit's outpouring of this love upon us we may have known, it is never enough!

Be Filled, and filled, and filled...

When D. L. Moody was once asked why he kept needing to be filled with the Holy Spirit again and again for his evangelistic work, his reply was simply, 'I leak!' There can be no greater outpouring of the Spirit than that which took place on the Day of Pentecost in Jerusalem (Acts 2), yet it is not long before we read of the Apostle Peter needing again to be 'filled with the Spirit' for ministry (Acts 4:8, 31). An awareness of our total inability to do this work does wonders for the prayer life!

No matter how gifted, knowledgeable, eloquent or charming we may be, we are all totally impotent and incapable on our own of doing anything of eternal worth. Charles H. Spurgeon says it perfectly, 'It is extraordinary power from God, not talent, that wins the day. It is extraordinary spiritual unction, not extraordinary mental power, that we need ... only spiritual power will save souls. What we need is spiritual power.'[37] We need fresh Holy Spirit power for each and every occasion. We need to be truly convinced that without Him we can do nothing but with Him, 'all things are possible'. The question is: are you desperate enough to be used, empty enough to be filled and humble enough to be led? Or are you content with the mundane, happy to be an *also ran* in life?

> There must be more than this
> Oh breath of God, come breathe within
>
> There must be more than this
> Oh breath of God, come breathe within
> There must be more than this
> Spirit of God we wait for You
>
> Fill us anew, we pray
> Fill us anew, we pray
>
> Consuming fire, fan into flame
> A passion for Your name
> Spirit of God, would You fall in this place?
> Lord have Your way, Lord have Your way with us
>
> Come like a rushing wind
> Clothe us with power from on high
> Now set the captives free
> Leave us abandoned to Your praise

Lord let Your glory fall
Oh Lord let Your glory fall

Consuming fire, fan into flame
A passion for Your name
Spirit of God, would You fall in this place?
Lord have Your way, Lord have Your way with us

Tim Hughes

7 God's Work and Ours

> I believe the doctrine of election, because I am quite sure that if God had not chosen me I would never have chosen him; and I am sure he chose me before I was born, or else he never would have chosen me afterwards.
>
> C. H. Spurgeon[38]

When engaged in evangelism or mission, we live continually under the dark cloud of temptation to discouragement. 'I'm no good at this.' 'We're doing something wrong here.' 'These people don't want to know.' 'There's no chance he will be saved!' These and other faith-dispelling thoughts can overwhelm us on those days when discouragements come tsunami-like, threatening to sweep us away from our area of service. I have found personally that the greatest motivation to persevere year after year in the work of evangelism is the biblical doctrine of God's election. Battle as we might at times with mysterious elements of this doctrine, it is hard for any Christian to deny its truth, and the fact that every true believer prays is a recognition and admission of the absolute sovereignty of God. As J.I. Packer points out, 'When we are on our knees, we know that it is not we who control the world.'[39]

Trinitarian salvation

Christians are unashamedly Trinitarian, rejoicing in the one God revealed in three Persons—Father, Son and Holy Spirit. All three Persons, therefore, must be involved in the work of salvation. In this context, the Apostle Peter brings the three into focus in one verse, speaking of our having 'been chosen according to the foreknowledge of God the Father, through

79

the sanctifying work of the Spirit, to be obedient to Jesus Christ and sprinkled with his blood.' (1 Peter 1:2). Arthur W. Pink points out, 'Election by the Father precedes the work of the Holy Spirit in, and the obedience of faith by those who are saved.'40 What confidence we can have in the gospel, then—a loving Father, an obedient Son, an indomitable Holy Spirit!

Sovereign Spirit

'The Father has sent his Son to be the Saviour of the world' (1 John 4:14) and then the Holy Spirit is the One sent to apply the saving work of Christ to the individual. He is the Sovereign Spirit whom no man or woman can entice to come or succeed in driving away against His will. In replying to the enquiring Pharisee, Nicodemus, Jesus teaches him this fact: 'The wind blows wherever it pleases. You hear its sound, but you cannot tell where it comes from or where it is going. So it is with everyone born of the Spirit.' (John 3:8).

It is the Holy Spirit who chases, then changes, people, supernaturally regenerating them and then immediately setting about His work of sanctifying them. This can be dramatic or not, happening to one or many. He can come as a warm, gentle breeze to one individual or like a mighty rushing wind to a multitude. He does whatever He wants, however He wants, whenever He wants. He is totally unpredictable; you never know what He might do next! So, if the Holy Spirit is sovereign over His work, we must seek to keep in step with Him as we labour together in the work of the gospel.

Cause of division

It has always been a grief to me that, historically, excellent men have divided over this truth, the clearest example being seen in the lives of those mighty evangelists John Wesley and George

Whitefield. Both were zealous 'men of action' who undoubtedly in their earlier years, when in the thick of battle, said and wrote things which inevitably would lead to their splitting into two distinct groups, Arminian and Calvinistic. In later years, both were saddened by the earlier bitterness that existed between them and although no merger of the two camps occurred, there was at least reconciliation between the leaders of the mighty eighteenth-century move of the Holy Spirit. Charles Wesley could write happily in 1755, 'Come on, my Whitefield! Since the strife is past ... friends at first are friends again at last.' On Whitefield's death, Charles penned a noble eulogy and, at Whitefield's request, his funeral sermon was preached by none other than his fellow evangelist in the great harvest, John Wesley.

It would be good to think that church history enables us to learn from past mistakes so that all who rejoice in the saving work of Christ pull together as one whenever possible, majoring on the essentials of the gospel. Today, of course, the battle lines are drawn not so much between Arminian and Reformed as between the Charismatic and non-Charismatic camps. Whilst avoiding the snare of ecumenism with its 'unity at the expense of truth', there must surely be areas where we can stand shoulder to shoulder in order to defend vital Christian truths and proclaim gospel essentials?

The battle is too fierce and foes too numerous for good people and churches to be divided unnecessarily. Besides our impact being weakened in our rapidly increasingly anti-Christian culture, millions are perishing without the basic truths of salvation through Jesus Christ alone. I have been deeply impressed and challenged over the years by George Verwer, who for sixty years has been motivating and harnessing thousands of people from a whole variety of cultures and theological backgrounds for the sake of the gospel through Operation Mobilisation, now one of the world's largest missionary organisations. This is no mean feat. But George is a gritty realist and only too aware of possible tensions. 'Where two or three are gathered in His name ... sooner or later there will be a mess!' he loves to say. (He expands on this theme in his humorously named, but tremendously serious book, *Messiology*.) It is no wonder when Paul admonishes us to '... keep the unity of the Spirit through the bond of peace', he prefaces his words with, 'make every effort' (Ephesians 4:3).

No Place for daggers!

Charles Simeon, the wise and influential vicar of Trinity Church, Cambridge, had little sympathy for mean-spirited Calvinists (surely an oxymoron for those who major on 'grace') and records a conversation he had with the elderly John Wesley on 20 December 1784:

> 'Sir, I understand that you are called an Arminian; and I have sometimes been called a Calvinist; and therefore I suppose we are to draw daggers. But before I consent to begin the combat, with your permission I will ask you a few questions. ... Pray, Sir, do you feel yourself a depraved creature, so depraved that you would never have thought of turning to God, 'I do indeed.' 'And do you utterly despair of recommending yourself to God by anything you can do; and look for salvation solely through the blood and righteousness of Christ?" "Yes, solely through Christ.' 'But, Sir, supposing you were at first saved by Christ, are you not somehow or other to save yourself afterwards by you own works?' 'No, I must be saved by Christ from first to last.' 'Allowing, then, that you were first turned by the grace of God, are you not in some way or other to keep yourself by you own power?' 'No.' 'What, then, are you to be upheld every

hour and every moment by God, as much as an infant in its mother's arms?' 'Yes, altogether.' 'And is all your hope in the grace and mercy of God to preserve you unto his heavenly kingdom?' 'Yes, I have no hope but in him.' 'Then, Sir, with your leave I will put up my dagger again; for this is all my Calvinism; this is my election, my justification by faith, my final perseverance: it is in substance all that I hold, and as I hold it; and therefore, if you please, instead of searching out terms and phrases and to be a ground of contention between us, we will cordially unite in those things wherein we agree.'[41]

Wesley himself refers to this conciliatory meeting in his Journals: 'I went to Hinxworth, where I had the satisfaction of meeting Mr. Simeon... He gave me pleasing information...'[42]

Every man and woman fully responsible

If it is God who elects, then how can God blame anyone for their sin? The Apostle Paul envisaged such an objection (Romans 9:19) and we too may have deep inner questionings. Is there not a bizarre contradiction here? J.I. Packer calls this an 'antimony'—that is, an appearance of a contradiction between two truths that seem equally logical, reasonable or necessary. 'To our finite minds this is inexplicable'.[43] However, Scripture clearly and unapologetically teaches both.

C.H. Spurgeon, when once asked if he could reconcile these two truths together, replied, 'I wouldn't try, I never reconcile friends.' It was obvious in the great preacher's sermons that he was comfortable preaching both God's election and also man's responsibility and culpability. 'This is the doctrine that we preach—if a man is saved, all the honor is to be given to Christ—but if a man is lost, all the blame is to be laid upon himself! You will find all true theology summed up in these two short sentences—salvation is all of the Grace of God—damnation is all of the will of man.' He preached this in a sermon in May of 1895,[44] but similar sentences can be found in various other messages of his.

It is plain to see the theology that shaped Spurgeon's mind and enlarged his heart in evangelistic preaching. He didn't merely pay lip service, but truly believed that God was not willing that any should perish but desired *all* to come to repentance. Spurgeon's total reliance on the sovereign Spirit in his preaching is evident also:

> The gospel is preached in the ears of all; it only comes with power to some. The power that is in the gospel does not lie in the eloquence of the preacher; otherwise men would be converters of souls. Nor does it lie in the preacher's learning; otherwise it would consist in the wisdom of men. We might preach till our tongues rotted, till we should exhaust our lungs and die, but never a soul would be converted unless there were a mysterious power going with it, the Holy Ghost changing the will of man. Oh Sirs! We might as well preach to stone walls as preach to humanity unless the Holy Ghost be with the Word to give it power to convert the soul.[45]

Gospel work can, at times, be heart-breaking work. We go to people with love-filled hearts, only to have the fire of devotion doused by cynical looks, unkind words—or worse. This, sadly, is par for the course. But how do we keep on going in the face of such testing to our faith?

As well as the physical sufferings Paul had to endure in seeking to reach the lost, there was also the emotional anguish of rejection, of being misunderstood, criticised and suspected. However, his words to young Timothy (significantly, among his final ones) reveal something of the motivation behind his tireless efforts through the years and what it was that sustained him when the sense of fear, failure or disappointment threatened to overwhelm him: 'Therefore I endure everything for the sake of the elect, that they too may obtain the salvation that is in Christ Jesus, with eternal glory.' [italics mine] (2 Timothy 2:10). He endured the opposition, attacks, beatings, imprisonment, rejection and long days of toil—for what purpose? We may have thought he might have replied, 'For the glory of God.' But he doesn't. Instead, he says he endures all of this 'for the sake of the elect.'

From cover to cover, Scripture reveals a triune God who sovereignly chooses and decrees and is especially clear in the area of salvation. He unashamedly declares, "'I will have mercy on whom I have mercy, and I will have compassion on whom I have compassion." It does not, therefore, depend on human desire or effort, but on God's mercy.' (Romans 9: 15–16). No-one emphasised the doctrines of election and the sovereignty of God more than the Apostle Paul yet, rather than this dampening his evangelistic zeal, we read his life is simply a blur of passionate, unceasing, frenetic missionary activity.

Having a firm grasp of election takes an awful weight off our shoulders in the area of evangelism and mission and provides us with enormous encouragement to continue to preach, witness and earnestly reach out to men and women, no matter how hardhearted they may appear at the time and how desperate a situation may seem from our human perspective.

Pam, the wife of one of the elders of a church I served in South Wales, was a Macmillan doctor working with cancer patients. Aware of the critical condition of so many of them, she knew that their greatest need was to know the Lord but was only too aware of the danger of overstepping professional boundaries. Seeking to be alert to the Holy Spirit's prompting and sensing that 'tug of the Spirit', Dr Pam would gently ask a patient, 'Would you like a visit from my pastor?' Because of her gracious approach, I was provided with numerous precious opportunities to speak of Christ to those who knew that their days on earth were few.

On one of those occasions I was asked to visit a man who had been moved into a side ward of the hospital for his remaining days. His was a hopeless situation, if ever there was one. I opened the door to see Ed, a large gaunt man with a grey pallor, lying in bed. As we spoke, I couldn't help noticing that in his bedside cabinet was a huge tome of a book about all the religions of the world. I knew very well his thoughts: 'I had better seek one of these out pretty quickly!' I took one look at the book and one at Ed and thought to myself, 'You're not going to have time to finish it!'

It is at moments like this that I thank God not only for the beauty and freeness of the gospel, but also for its simplicity. After explaining to him that he was loved by God, that it was not too late to get right with Him and that Christ had done all that was needed, I gave him a simple gospel tract and left. I called back a few days later, not knowing if Ed would be there or not. Slowly opening the door, I peered in and there was Ed, still grey and gaunt but with an enormous smile and eyes aglow with joy. I sat beside him and, taking my hand in his large hands, he said excitedly, 'I want to tell you what has happened!' But I already knew. A greater Visitor than I had been there and just in time, as within a few days Ed was gone. But his eternal destiny had been changed and to witness such a sight was yet another encouraging reminder for me personally that the Holy Spirit's call is like that of the

Lord Jesus when calling Lazarus from the dead: it is powerful, gracious, unpredictable and irresistible.

God's love for the non-elect

John Wesley is, without doubt, one of my heroes, but this mighty evangelist detested the doctrine of election—and often those who taught it—with a passion. He proclaimed, 'All the devices of Satan, for these fifty years, have done far less toward stopping this work of God, than that single doctrine. Be diligent to guard these tender minds against the predestinarian poison.'[46]

Perhaps one of the greatest reasons why Wesley rejected Calvinism was that he believed it taught that one was unable freely to proclaim the love of God for all men. This was a crucial and most unfortunate misunderstanding. Iain Murray points out: 'John Calvin himself had preached, "Jesus Christ offers himself to all men without exception to be their redeemer", and that "love... extends to all men, inasmuch as Jesus Christ reached out his arms to call and allure all men both great and small..."' Murray continues, 'The Puritans had no problem in speaking of "God's unspeakable love to mankind", or asserting that, "God hath general love to all the creatures."'[47]

God commands us to 'Be holy, because I am holy' (1 Peter 1:16; Leviticus 20:26). This means much more than attempting to live lives of moral purity, as the Pharisees sought to do. In His Sermon on the Mount, the Lord Jesus blows away their—and our—contracted concept of holiness in a number of areas. But perhaps the most devastating words of them all are in His teaching on love for one's enemies: 'You have heard that it was said, "Love your neighbour and hate your enemy." But I tell you, love your enemies and pray for those who persecute you, that you may be children of your Father in heaven. He causes his sun to rise on the evil and the good, and sends rain on the righteous and the unrighteous. If you love those who love you, what reward will you get? Are not even the tax collectors doing that? And if you greet only your own people, what are you doing more than others? Do not even pagans do that? Be perfect, therefore, as your heavenly Father is perfect.' (Matthew 5:43–48).

We are *commanded* to love our enemies. Do you think God would expect us to do something He Himself would not do? God loves those who hate Him, who would seek to harm Him or simply ignore Him and His claim upon their lives. The problem so often is that we find it hard—no, impossible—to obey this command. But we must ignore our feelings and inclinations, seeking to be like our Father in heaven who loves them and seeks to do them good—and ultimately the greatest good is in forgiving them their sin and rebellion.

We return again to our need of the Holy Spirit's power and grace to be at work within us, lifting us to a quality of life beyond that which is possible for fallen human beings. It must be stressed that it is *Hyper*-Calvinism which denies the love of God for every human being and therefore feels unable to offer the gospel freely to all—ironically, through fear of being unfaithful to God.

A problem today?

We might think that evangelicals in our day are not affected in any way by Hyper-Calvinism, but I fear that we are, more than we realise, and we can be guilty of being 'practical' Hyper-Calvinists. We might be tempted to think that this a nit-picking issue, but it is of utmost importance.

Firstly, if we have any doubt lurking within us that God has a love for all men and women then, when it comes to appealing to the unsaved, our language becomes stilted and wooden. There is a holding back, a distinct lack of a warm, overflowing declaration of God's love for those before us, through fear that they just might not be among the elect in the end.

Secondly, if we doubt God's love for all and His deep yearning for all to be saved, it will be evident in our evangelism—or, rather, our lack of it. Gifted and gracious pastor Robert Sheehan, in a paper given at the Carey Ministers' Conference on 'God's Love to the Non-Elect', began by saying, 'Increasingly, there is a tendency among a vocal minority within the Reformed tradition, not only to emphasise the distinguishing and electing love of God, but also to speak of the non-elect in such a disparaging way that the impression that they give is that God loves his elect and despises the rest!'[48]

We cannot doubt that the love of God for the elect, who alone benefit from the saving work of Christ, inevitably differs from that for the non-elect, but surely Sheehan touches on a raw nerve or two when he continues,

> As Jesus preached and healed all sorts of people, some who would believe and some who would not, the elect and the non-elect, he had compassion towards them because they were like sheep without a shepherd (Matthew 9:36). He did not look at the crowd with a distinguishing squint, with compassion on the elect but not on the non-elect! He had compassion on the crowd universally and promiscuously. This compassion to all, which so marked his words, was a regular feature of his ministry.[49]

Here is God incarnate, who by His words and actions plainly demonstrated a love for all who stood before Him.

Our Lord exhorted his disciples to love their enemies and do them good, not only because their reward would be great but also because by so doing they would be sons of the Most High, because He is kind to the unthankful and evil (Luke 6:35). We are to love our enemies because God loves His. His mercy is the pattern for ours.[50]

Experiencing the love of God ourselves

Although arguing from a subjective standpoint can be a dangerous practice, Iain Murray quotes Wesleyan John Nelson's powerful appeal: 'Tell me Sir, did you ever feel the love of God in your own soul? If you did, I appeal to your conscience, whether at that time you did not find love to every soul of man. Now, this was not your nature, but the nature of God; and if one drop of the bucket could so swell your soul, what must that ocean be from which it came?'[51]

Can the Saviour's sorrow and tears over unrepentant Jerusalem be understood apart from the indiscriminate love of God for all? Can the tears of a Spirit-filled Whitefield be understood as he is compelled to go outside and preach to the lost multitudes in the open-air, or the deep yearnings of the giant-hearted Spurgeon for the unsaved in his mega-church? Can the gracious gospel of our Lord Jesus Christ ever be presented with greater eloquence, no matter how stumbling and fumbling our words, than when we are filled with the love of God to such an extent that it spontaneously, meltingly, overflows to the hearer?

8 Overflow

It is said that in his preaching of both law and gospel, love 'was expressed in his every tone and movement, and could not fail to make an impression on their hearts'[52]

Spoken of Irish evangelist **Gideon Ousley**

There is something wonderfully contagious and expansive about the Holy Spirit's work in salvation. God changes one life and then a holy 'fallout' takes place. Perhaps silently, but unquestionably surely, the Hound of Heaven pursues and changes one person and then commences a contagious diffusion among others, spreading way beyond our ability to trace or calculate.

James Boice reminded us earlier of the phenomenal growth of the Early Church 'from Jerusalem (an obscure corner of the world) to Rome, the world's capital—all within a lifetime of the first generation of believers.' The death of Stephen, the first Christian martyr, was the catalyst, triggering persecution and dispersion of the church, then, Dr Luke informs us, 'Those who had been scattered preached the word [gossiped the gospel] wherever they went.' (Acts 8:4). The 'big guns' had been left in Jerusalem and it was 'the ordinary guys' who were the carriers of the good news—a brilliant reminder that we must never underestimate the power and potential of those who love Jesus and, as a result, simply 'overflow' and overflow simply.

Laura and Heidi, sisters aged eleven and nine years old, were trying to come to terms with what had happened to their dad. They saw him suddenly transformed from his increasingly observable addiction to alcohol into a joyful, enthusiastic Christian. Thankfully, much of the trauma had been hidden from them, but one thing was plain: the home was now a changed place! The rows between their parents and the tense atmospheres were now replaced with peace, harmony and happiness. The only downside they recall was being woken noisily for school each day by their 'new' father bringing morning cups of tea into their room, heartily singing 'Soldiers of Christ Arise'!

Laura's curiosity especially was aroused and two weeks later a visit of the Gideons to her school would bring about a change in her own life too, as she avidly read the New Testament and trusted the Saviour of which it (and her dad) spoke. The years passed and, now married and living in Canada with her children, all believers too, she is a Christian author and touches thousands of lives through her writings. Sister Heidi also came to trust the Lord and lovingly influenced lives as a cancer specialist nurse; shortly she will be joining her husband in full-time gospel work after his training for the Anglican ministry. Just how many cases are there of this gentle, but far-reaching dispersion of grace, this holy contagion? Nevertheless, there can also be the more overt examples, when the Holy Spirit works less like a breeze and more like a hurricane!

Helen Roseveare, a remarkable missionary who died aged ninety-one in December 2016, recalls how, when she was serving as a young doctor in the 1950s, God came suddenly in revival power to the then Belgian Congo. The dramatically transformed lives were rapidly to impact the surrounding area as a result:

> The first day revival came to Ibambi, the actual building shook. We were sitting in the Bible School hall. It was seven o'clock on a Friday night. Jack Scholes, our field

leader, had just come back from a trip in the south and he had seen revival down there. He stood up to speak about the revival and started to read from the Scriptures. Suddenly we heard a hurricane storm. It was frightening! We heard this hurricane coming and the elders began to take the shutters down—the shutters are not very strong and fall in and can hurt people. We looked out and it was moonlight and the palm trees were standing absolutely still against the moonlit sky. It should have been pitch-black and stormy. Then the building shook and the storm lanterns down the centre of the building moved around. There was a terrific noise and a sense of external power around. We were all frightened ... you could sense fear all around.

When asked about the first reaction to the presence of God among them, she replied,

Conviction of sin. People began to confess publically what you might call 'big sin' (and these were all Christians). They spoke of adultery, cheating, stealing, deceit. One friend, whom I thought too good to be true, was crying out to God for mercy and confessing her sins. I couldn't imagine she'd done anything wrong! We didn't leave the hall that whole weekend! Most of the time God was dealing with our sins. Some needed help from the pastors who moved around with much wisdom and encouragement. Then joy struck the repentant sinners and the pastors moved on.

Eternity became real to all affected by the Holy Spirit's presence. This was to have a significant evangelistic affect upon the revived Christians. Helen continues,

There were amazing visions of hell and people would break down weeping because of unsaved relatives. They carried exhausting prayer burdens. What started off as a ten minute prayer meeting lasted three hours. We didn't discuss anything; we spoke with God. There were waves of outpoured prayer.

Evangelistic teams were formed spontaneously:

Some went off at 4am on one occasion and walked twelve miles to a village, compelled by the Holy Spirit to share the gospel. Many were saved as a result.[53]

Missionary Spirit

Whether like a mighty rushing wind or as a breeze gently touching lives, the outcome resulting from a work of the Holy Spirit is exactly the same: others are inevitably affected by the overflowing witness of men and women who have met with, and been changed by, Christ. When the Spirit fills a person, 'overflow' is natural and spontaneous; there is an inner compulsion to pass on the good news, to take the life-saving antidote to those who are sick and dying. There is no need to coax or cajole people into speaking of Jesus.

It begs the question, however, why there is such a reluctance among Christians in the West to share the gospel today. Is it an indication that we are in desperate need of the Holy Spirit's power in the life of our churches and in our individual lives? The Holy Spirit is a restless missionary Spirit, ever pushing outward into all the world with the aim that every knee will bow and that every tongue confess that Jesus Christ is Lord, to the glory of God the Father. (Philippians 2:10–11).

Even as believers, our hearts are so sinful and slippery and we can satisfy ourselves that we have a desire for revival and to see God move, but our motives can be entirely self-centred. Leonard Ravenhill, as ever, causes us to wriggle with discomfort when he says, 'In revival, God is not concerned about filling empty churches, he is concerned with filling empty hearts.'

Revival overflow

J.I. Packer reminds us from church history of the natural overflow that takes place when the Holy Spirit is outpoured,

> Thus it was in the day of the Reformers, in the time of the Puritans, and during the evangelical awakenings that revived faith on both sides of the Atlantic in the eighteenth century. In those eras the gospel spread like prairie fire, not primarily because of the quality of the preachers but because lay Christians kept gossiping the gospel to their neighbours. And they did so spontaneously simply because they had been thrilled to the marrow by their own experience of God's salvation, which had made them into conscious lovers of Christ and heirs of heaven, no longer victims and prisoners of their pains and pressures—physical and mental, secular and religious—that threatened them on earth.[54]

'Irrepressible urge'

We stand always in need of a fresh work of the Holy Spirit in our personal lives, yet spiritual experience, if genuine, always looks outwards to the interest of others. It has an outcome—a glorious, compulsive, self-sacrificing overflow. A.W. Tozer speaking of this writes,

> Spiritual experiences must be shared. It is not possible for very long to enjoy them alone ... The irrepressible urge to share spiritual blessings can explain a great many religious phenomena. It even goes so far as to create a kind of vicarious transfer of interest from one person to another, so that the blessed soul would if necessary give up its own blessing that another might

receive. Only thus can that prayer of Moses be understood, 'Oh, this people have sinned a great sin, and have made them gods of gold. Yet now, if thou wilt forgive their sin—; and if not, blot me, I pray thee, out of thy book which thou hast written.' (Exodus 32:31–32). His great care for Israel had made him incautious, almost rash, before the Lord in their behalf … So it was in the Early Church and so it has always been when men meet God in saving encounter. They want to share the blessed benefits.[55]

Partnership with the Holy Spirit

We need to be realists and the stark truth is that we are totally incapable in our own strength of doing this work of making Christ known to a sometimes hostile, most times indifferent world. And God does not expect us to; He has designed that we partner Him.

The great Apostle Paul was only too aware of not being up to the job. 'Who is equal to such a task?' he cries (2 Corinthians 2:16). But he had that constant conviction that he was not alone in this task, but was sent with an authority and a strength not his own. 'We are therefore Christ's ambassadors, as though God were making his appeal through us. We implore you on Christ's behalf: Be reconciled to God.' (2 Corinthians 5:20).

Let us be clear, however, that when we use the term 'partnership in the gospel', we are not talking about equality! We dare never lose sight of our position before Almighty God. He is never our workmate, but our awesome Maker, Redeemer and Judge and we continue to stand before Him through sheer grace alone. Yet He stoops and condescends to work with us in bringing about His perfect will. This is a staggering privilege that we should never be able to get over.

And what greater encouragement can there be than when we comprehend that it is God Himself working with us, even within us, to bring about His purposes in salvation. Mark Dever reminds us how the heavy burden is lifted when we truly grasp this: 'In our evangelism we must be partners with the Holy Spirit, presenting the Gospel, but relying on the Holy Spirit of God to do the convicting and the converting.'[56]

Lifting up Christ

Betty Stam, who together with husband John, while they were only in their late twenties, paid the ultimate price for following Christ whilst seeking to make him known in China, beautifully expresses how simple and natural the task of evangelism and mission should be:

> No one can force a single soul or heathen to turn to Christ. All His followers have to do, all they can do, is to lift up Christ before the world, bring Him into dingy corners and dark places of the earth where He is unknown, introduce Him to strangers, talk about Him to everybody, and live so closely with Him and in Him that others may see that there really is such a person as Jesus, because some human being proves it by being like Him. That is positively all the Lord asks us to do for Him, because He himself does the rest.[57]

When we have grasped theologically that it is the Holy Spirit's work to convict and to convert and that He is the Sovereign Spirit, then we are released from being obsessed by the standard of our performance or our having to discover the right technique to use. It is the Holy Spirit working in and through willing men and women who love Jesus. And what greater adventure can there be, not knowing just where He might lead us next!

If we are sensitive to His leading, the Spirit will open unique doors of opportunity, just as in Acts 8:26–40, when Philip was surprisingly led out of a revival situation into a desolate desert place. He appears, right on cue, to answer the questions of an earnest seeker and place the final link in his salvation chain. William Wade comments on the evangelist's sensitivity and obedience: 'Philip left the relative ministerial fame of leading a revival in order to slip into seeming obscurity on the Gaza road. If ever there was an example of radical obedience to radical guidance, this was it. I wonder, would I do the same? Would you?'[58]

It is clear to see from the New Testament that the Holy Spirit is the Director of Evangelism and Mission. From His outpouring upon the church at Pentecost to the final page in the book of Acts, we see that it is He who both empowers and directs the followers of Christ in their task. We see Him leading into unusual divine appointments with individuals, as in Philip's case, to rubbishing perfectly reasonable plans and pressing the missionaries into a different direction altogether, the outcome being the formation of many churches in another continent, as the Apostle Paul experienced when seeking to take the gospel to Asia (Acts 16:6–10). 'The Spirit of Jesus' blocks their plans and re-directs them to Europe and after receiving a vision of a man of Macedonia appealing for help, they obediently set off and are led to the Roman colony of Philippi, where it becomes crystal clear that God has gone before them, preparing the way for the message to be received.

Divine delays

Of course, it all looks fine and cosy when, in a comfortable chair, coffee in hand, we read of gospel setbacks and delays, whether in Scripture or in Christian biography. But it is another thing when it is we ourselves who experience closed doors and crushing disappointment. We hear the anguish in Martha's voice when questioning the Lord regarding His delay in coming to her sick brother Lazarus "'Lord," Martha said to Jesus, "if you had been here, my brother would not have died." (John 11:21).

We must remember that God is not only concerned about evangelism, but also about sanctification; He is not only working through us, but *in* us! American author John Ortberg says that 'Biblically, waiting is not just something we have to do until we get what we want. Waiting is part of the process of becoming what God wants us to be.'[59] Many of us can testify to that painful intervening time between one door closing and another opening, but that is how faith and obedience are tested. It is so difficult for us to lay aside the slot machine mentality in Christian work: we do A and B and expect C to follow immediately. In the work of salvation, timing is everything and the fruit has to be ripe before it is picked.

The first meeting place for our fledgling church in Covent Garden was down a seedy West End back alley. We met in a room normally used for a homeless work and the atmosphere on Sunday mornings was usually pretty pungent. Looking out at the small congregation, I noticed a young man whose face was extremely scarred and who wore a black patch over one eye. As we spoke afterwards, he told me his story. James was a playwright and after his wife walked out he descended into deep depression, so much so that he saw no other way out but to take his own life.

Mercifully, things did not go to plan as he lay with his head in the oven and discovered that the gas was the kind that would not poison the system. Feeling he had failed even in this, he reasoned that he at least could cook a meal and eat something. However, as he bent down to light the oven the gas exploded, resulting in James receiving horrendous facial injuries. But here he was, on Easter Sunday, hearing the glorious message of One who looked death in the face but rose triumphant from the grave. Before leaving, he requested the loan of a Bible, remarking, 'This is my last chance.'

The real irony of the story is that James was given an invitation to our *Christmas* services! But God's timing was spot on and not many weeks later, as we knelt together, he surrendered his life to Christ in what I consider the most eloquent, yet broken, prayer of repentance I have heard a prodigal pray, complete with tears falling from below his patch. Although the surroundings were far from palatial, James in later days would always refer back to that 'sacred spot' where heaven came down and glory filled his soul as the great transaction took place and all heaven rejoiced as one sinner repented. One more precious prodigal came home.

Touched by loving hearts

Frances Crosby's hymn reminds us of the restorative power of the gospel when the love of Christ is communicated through those whom He has redeemed by His grace:

> Down in the human heart, crushed by the tempter,
> Feelings lie buried that grace can restore;
> Touched by a loving heart, wakened by kindness,
> Chords that were broken will vibrate once more.

'If anyone has material possessions and sees a brother or sister in need but has no pity on them, how can the love of God be in that person?' reasons the Apostle John searchingly (1 John 3:17). God's love for others must clearly manifest itself through His people in a genuine concern for the welfare of those in this world who are in need. We dare not say we have 'a love for souls' yet neglect the physical needs of those around us:

feeding the poor, aiding the immigrant, visiting the sick, freeing the addict, caring for the elderly, fighting for the unborn child, plus a hundred other things that scream out to us from our broken world.

Although we have a Saviour who came to 'give His life as a ransom for many' (Mark 10:45) and 'to do away with sin by the sacrifice of himself' (Hebrews 9:26), yet throughout His ministry He healed, fed and met the aching physical needs of the broken humanity that gathered daily before His pitying eyes. Tragically, the church does not have a good track record at holding evangelism and social concern in balance, at times having a heavy social action programme, but losing the gospel and at other times veering to the opposite end of the spectrum, holding 'faithfully to the Word', but failing to meet the glaring physical needs of men, women and children.

How encouraging it is to note the balance redressed in recent years. In the UK, Caring For Life and Christians Against Poverty are outstanding examples of how gospel proclamation and social concern can function so powerfully together, as well as there being a growing number of local churches following the same healthy pattern. Historically, the Holy Spirit seems to have been pleased to bless the evangelistic labours of those who cared for body as well as soul.

Leading up to the Welsh Revival of 1904-05, John Pugh, along with the Joshua brothers, Seth and Frank, was one of those whom God raised up and greatly used to stir Cardiff and further afield in South Wales. Pugh had a deep compassion for the poor of the city and organised the ladies of the church to go out with white flowers to give to the girls on the streets who, because of their poverty, had to sell themselves. Pugh remarked, 'I'm persuaded that a bird could as soon fly with one wing as the Church of God can evangelise the great centres of population without Christ-possessed women going out among the suffering poor.'

We must never think that the work of sharing the gospel is beyond any of us. Every Christian has all he or she needs only minutes after trusting Jesus Christ. Rebecca Manley Pippert helpfully reminds us that 'Our problem in evangelism is not that we don't have enough information—it is that we don't know how to be ourselves. We forget we are called to be witnesses to what we have seen and know, not to what we don't know...'[60]

It is never about our grasp of theology or how much of the Bible we know, useful as these are. Speaking of how sharing their faith was simply a way of life for the first followers of Christ, Roy Joslin said, 'Evangelism for the early Christians was not something they isolated from other aspects of Christian living in order to specialize, analyse, theorize and organise. They just did it!'[61]

It is not a matter of knowledge or technique, but a natural, authentic overflow of the life of Jesus outworked in the life of each person, each with their own unique personality and in their own particular environment. It is He, the Good Shepherd, who lovingly, diligently seeks the lost through those who have been found by Him and now have been enrolled to do that same work. A gracious manner is able to penetrate where the most eloquent words fail. The love of Christ is the most powerful force in the world and has an incredibly disarming effect upon the most hardened of hearts.

The evangelist John Wesley was often pelted with stones and dirt—and even with dead cats! He was a fastidious man who dressed in clerical robes throughout his ministry and no doubt did not delight in such opposition to him and his message as he stood to preach covered in mud and blood.

But the love of Christ within him produced a remarkable change in many of his adversaries. One day, yet another angry mob rushed toward him as he stood on a chair to preach. He records in his Journals, 'My heart was filled with love, my eyes with tears, and my mouth with arguments.' He then describes how a solemn hush came over the crowd, 'They were amazed; they were ashamed; they were melted down; they devoured every word.'[62]

A fragrance

The Apostle Paul says that 'we are to God the pleasing aroma of Christ among those who are being saved and among those who are perishing.' (2 Corinthians 2:15). In other words, the fragrance of our lives is pleasing to God, but it also attracts others to Him, or repels them. Smells are powerful in attracting us (a beautiful perfume) or repelling us (a sewer) and are difficult to ignore.

In the days of the Roman Empire, after a major victory in battle it was customary to celebrate before the citizens of Rome with magnificent parades. As a part of the ceremonies, fragrances and incense would be burned throughout the city as the armies marched through to the sound of triumphant music and the sweet aroma of victory. Even those who did not attend the parade could hear the music and smell the sweet aroma and they knew that Rome had been victorious. Paul speaks of Christians 'spreading everywhere the fragrance of the knowledge' of our precious Saviour. Amy Carmichael served with such devotion in India for over forty years and her beautiful life and writings still inspire thousands today. In her poem 'Fragrance' she encourages us to realise the potential and influence we 'earthen vessels' can have:

They say that once a piece of common clay
Such fragrance breathed as from a garden blows,
'My secret is but this,' they heard it say,
'I have been near a rose.'

And there are those who bear about with them
The power, with thoughts of Christ, men's hearts to stir;
For having knelt to kiss His garment's hem,
Their garments smell of myrrh.

So grant, I pray Thee, Lord, that by Thy grace
The fragrance of Thy life may dwell in me,
That as I move about from place to place,
Men's thoughts may turn to Thee.[63]

Of course, the downside is that we will at the same time be 'an aroma that brings death' to some. It was impossible for any who met Jesus to be neutral and it is no different today. Nevertheless, we must seek to be like Him and seek to cultivate what Spurgeon called 'the art of attraction': 'All spiritual fisherman should learn the art of attraction; Jesus drew people to him and we must draw them in like manner.'

In our cold, divided, self-centred and increasingly frightening twenty-first century world, we need not feel helpless nor be intimidated, but must simply seek day after day to bring something of the beauty and fragrance of Jesus to those within our sphere of influence.

Love which cannot be measured

Paul's earnest desire was that not only the Ephesian Christians to whom he was writing, but that 'all the Lord's holy people' might 'grasp how wide and long and high and deep is the love of Christ' and that we all may 'be filled to the measure of all the fullness of God' (Ephesians 3:18–19).

I know only too well when I am filled with such love and when I am not. When I am not, it is simply cold, cowardly, selfish, stupid Mike Mellor (my wife will supply you with a fuller list). But on those occasions when I am filled with the Spirit, it is then that I am, in some measure, how God wants me to be and I love Him and my fellow man in a way of which I am incapable of myself.

It is this love alone that delivered me instantaneously from alcohol addiction. I drove home that day in tears of joy, overwhelmed by the love of God, knowing He had forgiven me, knowing Christ had died for me, knowing that if I had a fatal car crash that day, I would go to heaven. But I was still on earth and was about to face a mystified wife!

Opening the door—she was in the kitchen—I called to her, 'Oh, Gwen, I've become a Christian!' Her head sunk into her hands and she gasped to herself, 'Oh, no. What's he up to now?' It was time to drive her to pick up her car from the garage where it was being repaired. On the way, I sought to further explain the inexplicable. We reached the garage and the mechanic presented me with the bill. 'Is that all it is?' I asked him. I wanted to pay him twice as much. I wanted to hug him (and he was ugly!). I loved him. I loved the whole world.

What on earth was wrong with me? Nothing. I, the guilty one, who fully deserved to be condemned to hell, had been freely pardoned and was on my way to heaven. I understood grace in a way which I think I've now forgotten. I loved all mankind and wanted all to be saved because I knew that God did. So, I set out to save the world.

9 Failure?

Sum up the life of Jesus by any other standard than God's, and it is an anticlimax of failure

Oswald Chambers[64]

I don't know if there is anyone who is entirely free from the nagging fear of failure. Given enough room to move, it has the potential to debilitate, even paralyse, the most confident among us. Kent Hughes, recalling his own 'dark night of the soul' at the start of his ministry, graciously admitted, 'I realised I had been subtly seduced by the secular thinking that places a number on everything. Instead of evaluating myself and my ministry from God's point of view, I was using the world's standard of quantitative analysis.'[65]

As Christians, we know the theory well enough and remind ourselves often that we 'walk by faith and not by sight' and that 'we are more than conquerors', etc. However, we are also creatures of time and space and in constant danger of losing perspective and the realisation of the eternal dimension to our faith. For this reason, we must ever be on our guard against the devil's master-weapon, discouragement.

Our enemy knows how we long to see the whole world saved and that we desire our short stay on this planet to have impact. But, in our efforts to win people for Christ, it is vital that at all times we are seeking to be obedient to the voice of the Holy Spirit, sensitive to being led by Him to the one or ones with whom He is presently striving. Like our Saviour, we long for 'all people to be saved and to come to a knowledge of the truth' (1 Timothy 2:4), but we must remind ourselves time and again that salvation is God's work and not ours.

Sowing and reaping

The most popular picture of evangelism in the Scriptures is that of sowing and reaping. Those reading would understand only too well that sowing was arduous and, at times, monotonous work, but well worth the labour because of the certainty of the outcome.

> Those who sow with tears will reap with songs of joy.
> Those who go out weeping, carrying seed to sow, will ['doubtless'(AV)] return with songs of joy, carrying sheaves with them. (Psalm 126:5–6)

Anyone involved in Christian work, whether Sunday School, door to door, sharing with a friend over coffee, Parent and Toddler group or whatever, will gain encouragement from this biblical picture. It is the certainty of a harvest that encourages the sowers to continue when the sun is hot, the back is aching and the brow is wet with perspiration. Gospel work is hard and, if we are truthful, at times boring work. For this reason, the Lord Jesus Christ told his Parable of the Sower—there *would* be an outcome for all our labours of sowing the Word:

> 'Others, like seed sown on good soil, hear the word, accept it, and produce a crop—some thirty, some sixty, some a hundred times what was sown' (Mark 4:20).

Avoiding devastation

The quickest way to fall prey to discouragement is to fail to recognise there is a process involved where patience and faith are essential qualities. Patience, because although we live in the age of the 'instant', God is never in a hurry. And faith, because we never ever really know what God is doing.

Laurence Singlehurst[66] speaks of how as a young man he led a mission in the north of Spain. He recalls how he and the students involved in the mission were certainly not lacking in the areas of enthusiasm and expectancy, being sure that faith alone was the key to cracking this particularly hard region. One month later, the outreach was over and when the four teams met up to compare notes as to how it went in their particular area, they were devastated to discover that not one person had come to the Lord. Singlehurst then began to notice the same bitter disappointment among other Christians in evangelistic work. This was a major watershed for him and this painful experience was invaluable in learning the importance of the process of sowing and reaping.

How reassuring it is to know that one may plant, another water, but it is God who causes the seed to grow and come to fruition (1 Corinthians 3:6) and our labour is never in vain. I don't know how many times, when engaged in open-air outreach, I have had Christians stop to speak a word of 'encouragement' like, 'It's good to see you out here doing this, brother—but does it work?' My response is always the same, 'Most don't want to know, but some always do!' On the toughest day I don't think I have ever returned home after an open-air session without sensing a 'tug of the Spirit' in some soul and on the best day there is the supreme joy of being able to lead to the Lord one who was 'ripe' for the kingdom.

Oh, yes, the gospel does work, but we must contribute our part in the process with patience and faithfulness, whether we see anything or not. Paul says, 'I planted the seed, Apollos watered it, but God has been making it grow. So neither the one who plants nor the one who waters is anything, but only God, who makes things grow. The one who plants and the one who waters have one purpose, and they will each be rewarded according to their own labour. For we are co-workers in God's service…' (1 Corinthians 3:6–9).

No fence

There are those people we meet who derive great comfort from the fact that they are 'sitting on the fence'. But there is no such fence. No-one can be neutral towards Jesus Christ. We are for Him or against Him, in the kingdom or outside, saved or lost, born again or not, wheat or chaff, in light or in darkness, on the road to heaven or to hell. The New Testament plainly speaks of two possible positions.

Claude Bennie, a dear friend of mine, was a gracious, faithful London City Mission evangelist, generally working alone in Central London for a number of years, seeking to win people for Christ. He was a real 'plodder'. One of his 'patches' was bustling Oxford Street, where he would daily spend hours offering tracts to the crowds from all over the world who flocked to the West End. One afternoon, he was approached by a cheerful American Christian tourist who asked him the question which any evangelist fears being asked: 'Say, brother, do you get many conversions in this work?' Claude, a measured, unhurried, droll Cornishman, stroked his beard and then, in his time, replied in rich West Country tones, 'No. I don't get many conversions. But I've had thousands of decisions.'

Swine?

We cannot, however, expect exemption from a broken heart when men and women reject Christ, walking away, sometimes laughing, choosing hell rather than heaven. To have a 'whatever!' attitude to the lost-ness of the lost reveals that we know little of the Saviour's burden and His Calvary love.

The gospels are rich with Christ's persuasive reasoning and tender pleading with the greatest sinners and hardest hearts, with the moral outcast as well as with the self-righteous Pharisee. And yet we are shocked to the core to hear Him say that there are some people we need to exercise special discernment over. 'Do not give dogs what is sacred; do not throw your pearls to pigs. If you do, they may trample them under their feet, and turn and tear you to pieces.' (Matthew 7:6).

To be sure, our mission is to take the good news from heaven 'to every creature', but Christ teaches plainly here that there will be occasions when we will be cheapening the precious invitation of salvation by offering it to them. We see Jesus refusing to speak to Herod (Luke 23:9) and Paul refusing to argue with those who resisted God's Word (Acts 13:44–49).

These are strong words, seeming even more severe when we consider the gracious lips from which they fell. But they forcefully drive home to us the terrible fact that there are solemn consequences for those who sling the grace of God back in His face. And there is more to consider besides their flagrant disregard for the gospel; such people can often be used by the evil one in having a detrimental, and at times devastating, effect upon those seeking to share the gospel.

Various characters have appeared at our open-air meetings, becoming 'regulars' and entering into conversation with team members. It became evident that, although their objections or attitudes may have varied, there was something dark about them. They were not simply entrenched in their views, but had a God-insulting manner. We discovered that those dealing with them could not only be spending hours in conversation, but afterwards felt as if their faith had received a severe knocking.

So we really do need to pray for Holy Spirit discernment in our conversations in order to recognise 'dogs' and 'swine' from those merely difficult people who perhaps may, in the future, 'come to their senses and escape from the trap of the devil, who has taken them captive to do his will'. (2 Timothy 2:26). We would do well to heed the wise words of George Bernard Shaw, who remarked humorously: 'I learned long ago, never to wrestle with a pig. You get dirty, and besides, the pig likes it.'

Resisting the Holy Spirit

'You stiff-necked people! Your hearts and ears are still uncircumcised. You are just like your ancestors: You always resist the Holy Spirit!' (Acts 7:51). Stephen's discourse is a great encouragement for preachers, indeed for all of us who seek to share God's Word. His message was biblical, anointed and well applied—but at the close he was stoned to death!

As a preacher, I find it an incredible comfort that there is no judging how good a sermon is from the response we receive. It really is irrelevant whether we receive approval, criticism or complete indifference. Ultimately, the question we must ask ourselves is, 'Was the message I sought to communicate approved by God?' It is a solemn fact that there may be those we encounter who, just like those listening to Stephen, will be resisting the Holy Spirit. No matter how clearly, wisely and winsomely you present the gospel to a person, there is just no penetrating their armour. Self-righteous and self-sufficient, they stubbornly refuse to allow God to speak to them through His messenger. Sadly, just as Stephen found, it is 'religious' people who are the worst offenders.

Charles is an outwardly deeply pious man whom I seem to wound each time I seek to preach the gospel in a certain town centre I visit. As soon as I open my mouth, as if by magic there he stands, right in my face, denouncing me. I suddenly feel so unofficial, dressed in my jumper and jeans, as the representative of the only true church towers over me in long black cassock, large pectoral cross around the neck, black cylindrical hat, black horn-rimmed glasses and sporting a long grey beard. He never tires of crying, 'Heretic!' Every effort to reason with him from the Scriptures slides Teflon-like off him.

But then, there may be that person who is not at all religious, but simply enjoys living a life of sin. When Paul was on trial before Felix he 'spoke about faith in Christ Jesus' and discoursed 'about righteousness, self-control and the judgment to come.' We read that 'Felix was afraid and said, "That's enough for now! You may leave. When I find it convenient, I will send for you."' (Acts 24:24–25). The Holy Spirit was at work in Felix's heart, but he was resisting the Spirit. He dismissed Paul and wanted to hear no more.

I was visiting door-to-door the area surrounding our church and a lady smiled nicely and dismissed me with the words, 'I don't have time for Him, thank you.' She was very polite, but quietly hostile towards the One in whose hands rest her life, her eternity. So we return to the importance of praying for Holy Spirit grace and discernment and for wisdom to know how to deal with the immortal being that is standing before us.

Blasphemy against the Holy Spirit

John Piper stated that

> The sweetest news for a sinner is that God has forgiven him, that God no longer holds his sins against him. But the worst news in the world is that God will never forgive you.' He then concluded his message with this helpful definition, 'The unforgivable sin of blasphemy against the Holy Spirit is an act of resistance which belittles the Holy Spirit so grievously that he withdraws forever with his convicting power so that we are never able to repent and be forgiven.[67]

The ongoing challenge for us in our work of evangelism is not only knowing what to say and how to say it, but to know when to stop saying it. The awesome truth is that there may be one standing right before us for whom it could be said, 'It would be better had they never been born'. This is the person (just like Judas, of whom these terrible words were spoken) who had opportunity after opportunity to respond to the gracious calling of the Holy Spirit throughout their lives. On occasion He may have spoken with a still, small voice and on others thundered dreadful warnings—powerful attempts using law and grace to awaken and save—but all to no avail.

If you are a person who worries if you have committed this sin, relax! The one guilty of blaspheming the Holy Spirit is never worried. That is just their problem. Fortunately, none of us has the gift of infallibility which enables us to see the eternal destiny of the one or ones standing before us. That would be a burden too great to bear. The encouraging fact is that there are those who externally seem impenetrable and unyielding when we bring the good news to them, but then, suddenly, we see the Holy Spirit effortlessly cause their walls to crumble and the King enters to take up His rightful residence.

Love is patient, love is kind

It was a tough day and I had just finished my open-air preaching. All throughout the message he stood there, tall, scowling, dressed completely in black with a pentagram choker around his neck. I handed out tracts to all those around who would take one, but stayed clear of the tall, moody young guy who continued to glare at me from a distance. Eventually, my cowardice overcome, I ventured towards him and, dry throated, croaked, 'Can I give you one of these?' 'I'm a bad boy', he warned me, swiftly adding that he had been forbidden entrance to a number of towns. Looking at his satanic pentagram, I asked him, 'How long have you been into Satanism then?' 'Years, mate. I rejected God at school, after I asked the RE teacher a question and he didn't answer.' 'What did you ask him?' I enquired. 'If there is a God, why do bad things happen?' he informed me. 'That was a good question. Do you mind if I have a stab at it?' I responded, with trepidation. 'Go for it, mate!'

Thankfully, before I entered into a Bible study on Genesis, he opened up even further and told me how from the age of three he had been beaten daily by his step-mother and abused by various people before eventually being taken into care. I changed tack and told him of the love of God found in Jesus Christ. Suddenly, his look softened, walls crumbled, frost melted and he opened like a flower. After a long, warm conversation (and Genesis study) my new best friend left with a Gospel of John and with a heart open to receive the next link in his salvation chain.

When speaking with individuals, the truth is we really don't have a clue as to what is going on inside. I still think of, and pray for, various people I have met over the years. What about the club owner? What was happening in that court room and our subsequent meetings? Was he resisting the Spirit? Blaspheming the Spirit? Will he be saved before leaving this world? The bottom line is, we just do not know who is guilty of this, the most serious of all sins, the blasphemy against the Holy Spirit. So we endeavour to plod on faithfully, keeping 'in step with the Spirit'.

10 Sensitivity to the Holy Spirit

Come, gracious Spirit, heavenly Dove,
With light and comfort from above;
Be our Guardian, be our Guide
Over every thought and step preside.

Simon Browne

We need to pay attention to the various ways Scripture pictures and symbolises the workings of the Holy Spirit:

Rain/water/rivers—speaking of the need of refreshing where there has been dryness and barrenness (Isaiah 44:4; John 4:14; John 7:37–39).

Fire—symbolising illumination, holiness, cleansing, judgement (Matthew 3:11, 12; Acts 2:3, 4; 1 Thessalonians 5:19).

Wind—signifying power, guidance (John 3:8, 20:22; Acts 2:2).

Oil—speaking of anointing, empowering (Isaiah 61:1; Zechariah 4:2–6; Acts 10:38).

Dove—representing peace and gentleness. The dove is a clean, sensitive creature. Surely it is significant that when the Son of God is baptised we read of heaven opening and the Spirit descending upon Him 'like a *dove*'. Then the Father's voice from heaven affirms His love for His Son, the sinless Prince of Peace whom He had sent to reconcile the world to Himself. (Matthew 3:16,17; Isaiah 9:6; 2 Corinthians 5:19). So it is vital that in our Christian life and service we are sensitive to the presence of the Holy One who indwells us.

Spirit of holiness

'It is God's will that you should be sanctified [holy]', the Apostle Paul writes (1 Thessalonians 4:3). Of course, he is addressing not only the Thessalonians, but all who are Christ's. I don't know about you, but every time I read verses like that, hear a sermon or read a book on holiness, I inwardly squirm, an alarm bell rings and a neon light flashes: 'FAILED!'

The very word 'holiness' can seem threatening and foreboding, throwing up pictures in the mind of black clothes, sour faces, utterly unattainable, even undesirable, targets. Michael Reeves hits the nail on the head, 'Without Christ, "holiness" tends to have all the charm of an ingrown toenail'.[68] I have to remind myself continually of certain biblical facts as to what is a holy life. When I do, then instead of running from God, I run to Him. A righteousness has been provided for me. I am a new creation. It is no longer I who live, but Christ who lives in me. A powerful Helper has been sent to live within. Holiness is living for, and living like, Jesus. If He hates sin, so do I; if He loves righteousness, so do I. I love Him because He first loved me—and, amazingly, still loves me.

The beauty of holiness

Puritan theologian, pastor and revivalist Jonathan Edwards helps to correct any skewed views we may have: 'Holiness is a most beautiful and lovely thing. We drink in strange notions of holiness from our childhood, as if it were a melancholy, morose, sour and unpleasant thing; but there is nothing in it but what is sweet and ravishingly lovely.'[69]

C.S. Lewis, writing two centuries later, emphasises not only the beauty but also the impact true holiness can have:

'How little people know who think that holiness is dull. When one meets the real thing... it is irresistible. If even 10% of the world's population had it, would not the whole world be converted and happy before year's end?'[70]

The 'felt' presence of God

We have a menacing enemy who is ever seeking to pull us to extremes. And perhaps there is no area of the Christian life where the devil is more active than in that of Christian experience. He knows only too well how vital an issue this is for our spiritual health and effectiveness. To live a life of stability and impact, we need to walk on two legs: doctrine and experience. If one is longer than the other, balance will inevitably be affected.

It is important, however, to distinguish between God's omnipresence and His special or 'felt' presence. Our omnipresent God is everywhere, all the time, in His universe, as we saw expressed by the Psalmist earlier:

> Where can I go from your Spirit?
> Where can I flee from your presence? (Psalm 139: 7)

When we speak of the 'felt' presence of God, we mean times when He manifests Himself personally or directly to a person or persons, or to a specific location, especially as evidenced in times of revival. We saw Helen Roseveare's experience earlier during her time in the Congo. Or we read Jonathan Edwards speaking of the change in the church and neighbourhood in New England in his day: 'The town seemed to be full of the presence of God; it was never so full of love, nor of joy, and yet so full of distress... it was a time of joy in families on account of salvation being brought to them—parents rejoicing over their children as new born, husbands over their wives, and wives over their husbands ....'[71]

We dare not consign this experience to the past or to the 'unusual'. Many people, during a time of crisis or bereavement, can testify to a measure of the Lord's 'drawing near' and their experiencing a 'peace that transcends all understanding' filling their hearts and minds. It cannot be explained in human terms; it is beyond human comprehension and explanation. It is His gracious 'felt' presence, sovereignly manifested in this way as 'the peace of God' (Philippians 4:7).

John and Betty Stam, the missionaries with the China Inland Mission martyred by the communists in the 1930s, would be the first to say that they were no 'super heroes'. But John's words reveal the hidden power of their lives when he wrote, 'Take away everything I have, but do not take away the sweetness of walking and talking with the king of glory!'[72].

The vital truth that every believer rejoices in, however, is that whether we feel Him or not, God is with us and we can trust Him even when there is no special sense given of His immediate presence. Nevertheless, surely it should be every Christian's desire to seek a close walk with our Saviour. 'Come near to God and he will come near to you', writes James (James 4:8). Therefore, it matters how we live.

Grieving and quenching the Holy Spirit

Unbelievers can resist and blaspheme the Holy Spirit. But it is only God's children, those redeemed by the precious blood of His Son and indwelt by the heavenly Dove, who are capable of the tragic acts of grieving and quenching Him whose presence we so desperately need.

Grieving the Spirit

Paul, writing to the church at Ephesus, commanded: 'Do not grieve the Holy Spirit of God, with whom you were sealed for the day of redemption.' (Ephesians 4:30). The Holy Spirit is not a force or an influence, but a Person who can be saddened by our behaviour. You can only grieve those who love you and eagerly desire your intimate company.

Paul proceeds in the following verses (31–32) to give examples of how we can do this and how we can avoid it. 'Get rid of all bitterness, rage and anger, brawling and slander, along with every form of malice. Be kind and compassionate to one another, forgiving each other, just as in Christ God forgave you.' Disharmony is sin and a breakdown in our fellowship with other believers (the context here) results in a breakdown in our fellowship with God and a forfeiting of His blessing.

Whilst seeking to reach out to lost men and women, it is essential that we are on our guard, ensuring we are not foolish enough to engage in God's work whilst in a state of having 'shooed away' the gracious Dove, whom we so desperately need to accompany us. The Dove and the uncleanness of sin can never dwell together. We choose to have the presence of one or the other. Besides wounding the God we love, sin has a terrible hardening, pharisaic effect upon our hearts—fatal when seeking to reach sinful men and women for Christ. Tenderness of heart is never an optional grace for us.

Reminding us of the people we need to be, Roger Carswell urges, 'We are to speak from the inmost passion of our heart, but to do so with winsome care, recognising that people have been wounded by the society in which they live, and blinded by the enemy of their souls.' Roger quotes John Watson, a nineteenth-century theologian, 'Be kind, you do not know what battles people are fighting.'[73] We go to a 'wounded' people who are in need of gentle handling on the part of those indwelt by the Dove. It was said of the great evangelist George Whitefield that he rarely preached without tears and that people always sensed that he loved them and sought their good, even if he had hard things to say.

Quenching the Spirit

Paul is writing now to the saints at Thessalonica, instructing them: 'Do not quench the Spirit.' The symbolism has changed from friendship to fire and, just as a fire can be quenched, the promptings of the Holy Spirit can be smothered and stifled by Christians.

It might be asked, 'What is the difference between grieving and quenching the Holy Spirit?' I would say, that after graciously seeking time and again to get the attention of a believer, but in vain, the Holy Spirit gives up trying. That person is still a Christian, but he or she has missed out on being used by God. Grieving has turned into quenching.

Perhaps the Spirit has been prompting you over a certain matter—to set aside time to seek Him in prayer, to serve in the church, to visit someone, to do an act of kindness, hand out tracts, to send someone a card of encouragement, to make a phone call, whatever it might be—but you have ignored His voice and He is quenched and will simply by-pass you and use someone else. The job will get done, but you will be the loser.

How many Christians are simply 'deadwood'—'pew fodder'— in the church? The real tragedy is that they no longer care, they have become increasingly deaf to the Spirit's voice and promptings. Now they are anaesthetised and neither the Scriptures nor the most powerful sermons touch them anymore. Oh, yes, they have a testimony, but it is always in the past tense and they share it with you unblushingly: 'Oh, I used to give out tracts/used to share my faith/used to visit the elderly, etc.' Christian, don't get there!

Listening for the Spirit's voice

Being sensitive to the Holy Spirit means eagerly listening for His voice in order to do His will. Martyn Lloyd-Jones linked failing to do this with quenching the Spirit.

> Here again is a most extraordinary subject, and indeed a very fascinating one, and from many angles, a most glorious one. There is no question but that God's people can look for and expect 'leadings', 'guidance', 'indications of what they are meant to do'. There are many examples in the Scriptures [He then refers to Philip the evangelist and the Ethiopian in Acts 8.] Now there are leadings such as that. If you read the history of the saints, God's people throughout the centuries, and especially the history of revivals, you will find that this is something which is perfectly clear and definite—men have been told by the Holy Spirit to do something; they knew it was the Holy Spirit speaking to them, and it transpired that it obviously was His leading. It seems clear to me that if we deny such a possibility we are guilty of quenching the Spirit.[74]

At the very heart of evangelism are those 'divine appointments'. What is evangelism? It simply is the one who has the message being brought into contact—at just the right place, at just the right time, saying just the right things—with the one who is prepared to receive the message. We need not become mystics, afraid to move and do anything unless we hear 'a voice' telling us, but we need to go about our secular work or regular spiritual commitments with the prayerful expectation that God will lead us to make the 'right moves' when we need to. William Wade, an evangelist to the British Forces with SASRA, testifies:

> If I simply go somewhere to see what might happen, the regular outcome is that nothing happens: no opportunities to witness, no in-roads for the gospel, no testimony of God at work. Yet if I walk around the military barracks where I work, praying for God to send me to the right person or people; drop into a place where I know soldiers will be; or do my usual rounds of visiting the troops in their blocks in the evenings with gospel intentionality—then it should come as no surprise that God does open doors of opportunity.[75]

It cannot be stated too strongly that the Holy Spirit's 'leadings', to use Lloyd-Jones' phrase, will never contradict the Word of God. The two will always be in complete harmony and agreement. This does not mean, of course, that we cannot expect God on occasions to do the unusual and the remarkable. We dare not limit Him or box Him into our neatly packaged theological framework.

In 1908, two new missionaries, John and Jessie Perkins, were convinced that God had led them to Africa, but didn't know exactly where. Seeking to be obedient, they bought tickets and boarded a steamship circling the coast of Liberia, trusting that God would guide them in knowing where to get off. When the ship rounded Garraway Point, they strongly sensed the Holy Spirit's leading to get off the ship at this point. They had no idea that a young man named Jasper Toe lived in this region. He was God-fearing, yet practised religious rituals and had never heard the name of Jesus. One night he looked up to the heavens and prayed, 'If there is a God in heaven, help me find you.' That very night he sensed

God speaking to him. 'Go to Garraway beach. You will see a box on the water with smoke coming out of it. And from that box on the water will come some people in a small box. These people in this small box will tell you how to find me.'

Jasper went seven days by foot to Garraway beach, arriving on Christmas Day. He saw the box (a steamship) floating on the water with smoke coming out of it at the exact time when John and Jessie sensed God telling them to get off their boat. When they approached the captain of the ship, he was reluctant to let them off, informing them that it was cannibal territory and that people who went there didn't come back. John was adamant: 'God wants us to get off the boat.' In a canoe, with all their belongings, this brave couple headed to shore in a small 'box'. Who should be on the shore to meet them but Jasper Toe. He took them to his village where they eventually learned the language of his people. They started a church and Jasper Toe was the first convert. His life was changed—and all could see it.

H.B. Garlock, missionary and former Regional Director for the Assemblies of God in Liberia, described Jasper Toe as the godliest man he had ever met. Jasper became the first AOG General Superintendent and his own personal confirmation regarding this gracious work of the Holy Spirit in his beloved Liberia would be the hundreds of churches that he had been involved in establishing. All this started with the bare obedience of one couple who had an open ear to God.[76]

Sanity and expectancy

Maintaining a balanced view in any area of the Christian life is always difficult. Lloyd-Jones said that is can be compared to a man walking on a knife-edge, with the possibility of easily falling on either side.[77] Being sensitive to the Spirit's voice does not mean throwing away our discernment or common sense. Continually waiting for remarkable supernatural Holy Spirit guidance will make us either spiritually inactive for most of the time or else turn us into nervous wrecks.

But, surely, we desire to maintain an open ear to hear His voice? Sadly, as the years pass, we can become deaf to it if we are not careful, resulting in our ending up dull, dry, tame and predictable because our God has become just that to us. Either side of the knife-edge, fanaticism or deadness await us, but walk its narrow path we must if we wish to stay alive and effective.

Practically, perhaps we need to prayerfully start each day as Allen Baker does:

> Each morning, in my personal devotional time, I pray something like this, 'Good morning Holy Spirit. I ask You to fill me today, I ask that You direct my path and bring me into contact with someone who needs Jesus. If You open the door for gospel conversation, then I will go through it. And when I preach today, I ask, Holy Spirit, that you fill me, empower me. I need Your anointing, Your unction on my preaching, on my life and ministry. I have nothing to offer in my flesh. I can do nothing apart from You. So please come upon me and empower me for Your glory. Open my mouth and fill it with Your word.' And I find myself praying this repeatedly through the day.[78]

11 Joyful Obedience

At God's command I left all that is usually thought to make life worth living ... and have been called fool and fanatic again and again

C. T. Studd[79]

The word 'obedience' immediately brings a sour taste to the palate of most in today's 'free-thinking' culture. Although it is something we know is expected of us, it is given grudgingly and rarely without an inward resistance, beaten only in the unpopularity stakes by its buddy, 'submission'. However, followers of Jesus Christ see the word in an altogether different light because we know that obedience and joy are intimate friends.

The very purpose for which we were created is to obey and *enjoy* our Maker. As *The Shorter Westminster Catechism* succinctly states, 'Man's chief end is to glorify God, and to enjoy him for ever.' The hosts of heaven see this perfectly and declare it in this rapturous hymn of praise:

> You are worthy, our Lord and God,
> to receive glory and honour and power,
> for you created all things,
> and by your will they were created
> and have their being.
> (Revelation 4:11)

To live for the glory of Him who made us is to live as God created us to live. Conversely, to pursue happiness in life whilst living in disobedience to God is the sure way to a life without true happiness and, sadly for many, the quick route to depression. The Lord Jesus Christ explains in a sentence how obedience and joy are linked: 'Anyone who loves me will obey my teaching. My Father will love them, and we will come to them and make our home with them.' (John 14:23). He is saying, in so many words, 'If whilst living on this sin-cursed planet you want to capture something of heaven (that is, dwelling in God's presence) then obey My teaching.'

Spurgeon speaks of the struggle we so often have in surrendering our will to God's, as though we were somehow going to lose something. He eloquently, as ever, directs us to the pathway of true happiness:

> Ah, brothers, it is hard to say, 'Not my will, but Yours be done.' But we must say it ... What do I desire when I wish to have my own will? I desire my own happiness! Well, I shall get it far more easily if I let God have His will, for the will of God is both for His own Glory and my happiness! ... The only way in which this can be attained is by the unction the Holy One, the outpouring and the indwelling of the Holy Spirit in our hearts.[80]

Could it be possible that you have arrived at a point in your Christian life where you no longer expect to hear the voice of God speaking to you in a personal way? There is no longer any room for risk or uncertainty. To ensure you are safe, you have 'tamed' those dangerous areas that once scared but also thrilled you. It has been a gradual process, no doubt, but for some years now you have been keeping God at arm's length and as a result have been slowly dying. Mike Yaconelli, seeking to help us recognise the tragedy of the situation, writes,

> How could we begin our lives with clarity and passion, wonder and spontaneity, yet so quickly find ourselves at the middle or end of our lives, dull and bleary-eyed, listless and passionless? The death of a soul is never quick. It is a slow dying, a succession of little deaths.[81]

The Apostle Paul reminds us that joyful obedience is our natural response to the cross of Jesus Christ and is the *normal* Christian life and experience: 'Therefore, I urge you, brothers and sisters, in view of God's mercy, to offer your bodies as a living sacrifice, holy and pleasing to God—this is your true and proper worship.' (Romans 12:1). Yaconelli, speaking from his own painful experience, bares his heart and describes how, after years in a spiritual wilderness, he met afresh with God and '... the numbness of my soul began to dissipate'. He adds, 'He has not protected me from the dangers of living, but has led me into the dangerous place of wild and terrifyingly wonder-full faith.'[82]

Do we not, every one of us, stand in desperate need of a fresh vision of the beauty, majesty and terrifying power of the Jesus we profess to know and serve? But perhaps there is a barrier to be removed. Dear friend, if you are struggling to surrender your all, then why not ask the Holy Spirit right now to make you willing to be willing? Put down this book and pray. You can be sure it is a prayer God delights to hear and answer.

Soul-stirring question

I was released from alcohol's unyielding grip in a split second. One taste of heaven's joy and I knew instantly that this was the thing I had really thirsted for all those years, but of which I had lived in total ignorance. I still ask why it took thirty-one years before anyone told me! I knew very little as a rookie Christian, but one thing I was totally convinced of: joy and obedience are inseparably fused, so, as a result, I proceeded in my spiritual infancy to ransack the Scriptures and devour Christian books.

One night, whilst still working as a musician, I sat reading a book in between the two shows, in the band room of the theatre in which I was working. It was *The Passion for Souls*, written by the Canadian evangelist Oswald J. Smith. In this particular chapter he was recounting the outpouring of the Holy Spirit upon a nineteenth-century evangelist in North America who had changed all his plans (en route to pick up his fiancée to be married!) in order to remain where God wanted to use him. Then came the question, 'How many, I wonder would do that? How many would be willing to turn aside from their own plans and obey the Spirit of God?'[83]

My heart leapt and I cried, 'I will!' It was as if I had been struck by lightning. I could barely lift my trombone to play the second performance. I knew God had spoken and I simply wanted more of the joy that accompanied obedience to Him.

It is this position I have sought to maintain, no doubt very imperfectly, throughout the thirty-six years that have followed, regardless of pressures of family, finances or any fears that may concern me. I want the joy of the Lord and to know His smile more than anything else. Undoubtedly our lives will be littered with blips and inconsistencies, but it is the 'set of our sail' which determines the direction in which we travel, so we ensure that we achieve this by seeking to live in ready response to God's voice. Perhaps I could put Smith's challenge to you? 'Would you be willing to turn aside from your plans and obey the Spirit of God?'

Simon Guillebaud is a young man who obeyed the voice of the Holy Spirit, leaving his job in marketing and living today on the edge in war-torn Burundi with his wife and children, heading up Great Lakes Outreach. His joyful obedience is contagious as he invites us to receive by giving and conquer by surrendering:

> God calls people to all sorts of vocations. He longs to harness the gifts he's given us for use in his service. The

crucial factor is that he calls us all to full surrender. In my case this life of surrender has taken me to Central Africa. That has meant living in a war zone ... Although few live in such extreme circumstances, all of us are involved in a spiritual war zone. There's a battle going on for our hearts. What I watch and listen to, what I spend my time and money on—all these things have an impact. God wants our everything—not to limit us or stop us enjoying life, rather to release us into his appointed calling. If he gave everything for me, and knows what's best for me, then surely it makes sense to give my all back to him, to use for his purposes and glory.[84]

In his book, *Don't Waste Your Life*, John Piper seeks to stir within us a yearning for our one life upon this planet to have eternal impact: 'Desire that your life count for something great! Long for your life to have eternal significance. Want this! Don't coast through life without a passion.'

C.T. Studd joyfully exchanged his family fortune and fame as an England cricketer for a life of obscurity and poverty as a missionary, but there was never a happier man. 'At God's command I left all that is usually thought to make life worth living... and have been called fool and fanatic again and again.'

Some years later, Jim Elliot, a young American, replied to those who would have criticised Studd's mentality with those now memorable and oft quoted words, 'He is no fool who gives what he cannot keep, to gain what he cannot lose.' He lived out what he preached, being speared to death aged twenty-eight whilst seeking to reach the Auca Indians with the gospel, leaving behind a wife and young daughter.

This past year, Alistair and Anna Youren, a young couple in my own church, recently left the comforts and security of life in the West and, together with their two young children, are serving the aboriginal Yolgnu people of Arnhem Land with Mission Aviation Fellowship. In a recent prayer letter, they write of the hopelessness when witnessing so many lives being ruined by drink and drugs and the heartache of seeing children stealing their aviation fuel to sniff. Yet, in virtually the next breath, they tell of the boundless joy as Scriptures are delivered, hungry souls snap them up and a large number profess faith in Christ.

Is it worth it?

Ours is a materialistic culture where we are bombarded constantly by voices telling us loudly and persistently to 'walk by sight and not by faith' and to 'store up for yourselves treasures on earth". (compare 2 Corinthians. 5:7; Matthew 6:19). Consequently, we want our reward now and want to see something now for our labour. It's not surprising, then, that living in a culture, even in the church, which looks for its heaven in this life, the question is asked (if not vocally, then certainly voiced within) 'Is it really worth it?' 'Is it worth the money and effort expended, the lives wasted?'

Elizabeth Elliot replies

When asked this question, Elisabeth Elliot, widow of Jim, replied:

> Was it worth it? Does it make sense that five men with those kinds of qualifications should die for the sake of sixty people? By whose standards can we answer that question? Well, we say, lots of Auca Indians got saved. I've heard stories of thousands of volunteers to the mission field. I'm not sure if they're there today. I know there are some. People everywhere tell me they were moved and changed by the story. Hundreds of young men have told me that the book, 'The Shadow of the Almighty', changed their lives. I don't deny that for a

moment. Suppose it's all true—does that make it worth it? Let's suppose for a moment that not one Auca Indian got saved, that not one person ever heard the story of those five men, let alone was changed by it. Would it be worth it?

Then she continued,

Yes! Yes! Why? Because the results of my obedience to God are the business of God Almighty who is sovereign. It is the love of Christ which constrains us. There is no other motive for missionary service that will survive the blows of even the first year. We do it for Him.[85]

Helen Roseveare replies

Helen Roseveare, whose experience of revival in the Congo we looked at earlier, was confronted with the same haunting question. The setting is Columbia Bible College campus in South Carolina, where she is asked to share her experiences as a missionary to a visibly uninterested male audience. One of them recalls witnessing the now elderly Helen that evening:

Simple cotton dress. Grey hair pulled back in a bit of a bun. Very thick, coke-bottle glasses, because her eyesight was not good. And she was tired. So somebody grabbed a grey, folding, metal Samsonite chair and put it in the middle of the floor, and, and, and she sat on it, and they said, 'Gentlemen, this woman, Dr. Roseveare, has just come through our campus, we just want her to share a little bit of her experience with you tonight.'

And so she started to give her testimony. And being the astute woman that she is, about two minutes into her testimony, she knew that most of those guys were not interested at all, and so she stopped. And she said, 'You know what, boys, I don't want to bore you with the details of my life. You've probably heard different stories and so forth. So, it's late, why don't we just take another five, ten minutes or so and, and I'll just answer questions. Maybe, you know, you have a question, I'd rather talk about the things you're interested in.'

And this kid immediately stuck his hand up, I feel sorry for him to this day, he stuck his hand up, then said, 'Yeah, I've got a question. You know, we've got missionaries coming through here all the time, and, they're always talking about, you know, paying the price and suffering for Jesus—what did you ever suffer for Jesus?' She sat there and looked at him and, without any bitterness or any anger, she said, 'Well, during the Simba Uprising, I was raped twice.'

Everything got real quiet. And then she told us about the rape. She told us how the government soldiers came to her bungalow that night, came inside, ransacked it, grabbed her, beat her, threw her to the floor, kicked in all of her teeth. And then two army officers, one at a time, took her to her own bedroom and violated her body by raping her. And then, after the second incident, she was dragged from that bungalow out into a clearing and tied to a tree. And standing around the tree were all the laughing government soldiers. And then, while she was standing there, beaten and humiliated and violated and ridiculed, someone discovered in the bungalow the only existing hand-written manuscript of a book that she had been writing about the Lord's work in the Congo over an eleven year period. They brought it out, put it on the ground in front of her, and burned it. And as she saw that book go up in smoke, through clenched teeth she said to herself: 'Is it worth it? Is it really worth it? Eleven years of my life poured out in selfless service for the African people and now this.'

And then she told those boys in that dormitory room that night as we all sat there spellbound, she said, 'And boys, the minute I said that, God's Holy Spirit settled over that terrible scene, and He began to speak to me, and this is what He said. He said to me: "Helen, my daughter Helen, you've been asking the wrong question all your life. Helen, the question is not, 'Is it worth it?' The question is: 'Am I worthy? Am I, the Lord Jesus who gave His life for you, worthy for you to make this kind of sacrifice for me?'"' And by her own tearful testimony she told us how God broke her heart, she looked up into the face of Jesus and said, 'Oh Lord Jesus, yes, it is worth it, for Thou art worthy.'[86]

Suffering and success

The Apostle Paul warns that, '... our struggle is not against flesh and blood, but against the rulers, against the authorities, against the powers of this dark world and against the spiritual forces of evil in the heavenly realms.' (Ephesians 6: 12). He seeks to drive home the fact that every church and every Christian is inescapably involved in a cosmic spiritual warfare. There is a blood-earnest fight to be fought and ground will rarely be taken for the kingdom without casualties.

In any gospel work, in any part of the world, there is always a price to pay and on a personal level no soldier of Christ will emerge from life's battle without scars. This is the very nature of New Testament Christianity—and we must never think that the Holy Spirit will steer us away from trouble. In fact, in so many cases, He leads us along the road to ultimate victory right through the centre of the thorny territory of suffering and conflict— but it is the road to victory and to genuine 'success'. Paul, in his own ministry, recognised and gladly embraced this fact. Despite those who loved him and would have wished to have deterred him, he said, 'And now, compelled by the Spirit, I am going to Jerusalem, not knowing what will happen to me there. I only know that in every city the Holy Spirit warns me that prison and hardships are facing me. However, I consider my life worth nothing to me; my only aim is to finish the race and complete the task the Lord Jesus has given me—the task of testifying to the good news of God's grace' (Acts 20:22-24).

When American Baptist missionary Adoniram Judson first arrived in Burma, nobody had ever heard the name of Jesus. When he died, there were 7,000 baptised Karen willing to live or die for Christ. But, as his biography graphically records, it was not without enormous personal cost. In later years, their son Dr Edward Judson, at the dedication of a large church building in New York City, highlighted the unavoidable connection in gospel ministry between success and suffering, 'Suffering and success go together. If you are succeeding without suffering, it is because others before you have suffered; if you are suffering without succeeding, it is that others after you may succeed.'

No scars?

The Apostle John writes in his first letter, 'Whoever claims to live in him must live as Jesus did.' (1 John 2:6). Amy Carmichael, in her poem 'Hast Thou No Scar', poignantly highlights the inevitability of wounds for all who seek to follow in the Master's footsteps:

> Hast thou no scar?
> No hidden scar on foot, or side, or hand?
> I hear thee sung as mighty in the land;
> I hear them hail thy bright, ascendant star.
> Hast thou no scar?

Hast thou no wound?
Yet I was wounded by the archers; spent,
Leaned Me against a tree to die; and rent
By ravening beasts that compassed Me, I swooned.
Hast thou no wound?

No wound? No scar?
Yet, as the Master shall the servant be,
And piercèd are the feet that follow Me.
But thine are whole; can he have followed far
Who has nor wound nor scar?[87]

Our task

We are Christ's witnesses for today and have been sovereignly called to serve Him at this particular time in history. Being a follower of the Crucified has never been easy and it never will be. But we fix 'our eyes on Jesus, the pioneer and perfecter of faith. For the joy set before him he endured the cross, scorning its shame, and sat down at the right hand of the throne of God.' (Hebrews 12:2). God has designed it that joy and the cross belong together.

During China's Boxer Rebellion of 1900, rebels captured a Christian mission station and blocked all the gates but one. In front of that one gate, they placed a large cross flat on the ground. Word was passed to those inside that any who would be willing to trample the cross underfoot would be permitted to live and be set free, but any refusing would be shot. Terrified, the first seven students trampled the cross under their feet and were allowed to go free. But the eighth student, a young girl, refused. Kneeling beside the cross in prayer for strength, she rose and moved carefully around the cross—and then went out to face the firing squad. Inspired by her courage, every one of the remaining ninety-two students followed her, to the firing squad.

I wonder how much of today's gospel success among the Chinese today is owed to individual acts of faithfulness and sacrifice, as well as to the heroic 'seed-sowing' of missionaries like Robert Morrison, Hudson Taylor, William Burns and John and Betty Stam? 'Very truly I tell you', said our Saviour, 'unless a kernel of wheat falls to the ground and dies, it remains only a single seed. But if it dies, it produces many seeds.' (John 12:24).

It is surely significant that the Chinese church today is one of the most powerful missionary forces in the world. An article in a missions magazine about the impact of these Chinese believers stated: 'The Chinese may not wear traditional clergy clothing or be graduates from recognised seminaries, but God's Spirit is moving them...' It then mentions the biggest difference between Chinese and Western churches: 'Western churches see missions as extracurricular activity, Chinese see it as the most essential element of their existence.'[88]

Unstoppable gospel

The glorious fact is, the gospel cannot fail; it is unstoppable, simply because God is unstoppable and His sovereign Spirit is powerfully at work in the world. The question is: Are you available for Him to use? You may not have received a call from God to go to the mission field, but all are under orders from King Jesus to 'go to the ends of the earth' as His witnesses. Exactly where we are planted differs, naturally. But wherever He plants us, we are to be fruitful.

Although a mega-church pastor in the States, Bill Hybels has a real heart for the 'ones' and recalls how his life was transformed by 'just a walk across the room'. He speaks of the transformation that followed a prompting of the Holy Spirit to overcome his reluctance and, in obedience, simply crossing a room to talk to a Muslim man who, it transpired, had a hungry, searching heart.

Hybels speaks about the enormous impact that one act had upon his own life. 'My heart and mind awakened afresh to personal evangelism. The insight God would give me after interacting with this man would shed new light for me on how the Holy Spirit moves in the lives of Christ-followers when they commit to staying in vibrant, dynamic fellowship with God.'[89]

Ready and Waiting

Each and every Christian has been commissioned to represent Jesus in this fear-filled, hopeless world and to speak of Him to our perishing generation. They have no-one else. Whether it means crossing the room, the road or the globe, we all are on a mission.

We can be in no doubt that we all, without exception, desperately need more of the Holy Spirit's power in our lives. No matter what measure you have of Him (or Him of you), there is more! But He is the sovereign Spirit, whom we can neither control nor manipulate and we are again reminded of the importance of the 'set of our sail', being prepared so that when there is a blowing of that holy wind, we are in a position for take-off. Amy Carmichael had two words written on the wall of her room: 'Yes, Lord'. Her sail was set.

I have personally found certain prayers an encouragement in this area. They (if I may change the metaphor) help to make me 'ignitable' for the flame of the Spirit to set my icy heart alight.

The Covenant Prayer of John Wesley

I am no longer my own, but yours.
Put me to what you will, rank me with whoever you will.
Put me to doing, put me to suffering.
Let me be employed for you or laid aside for you,
exalted for you or brought low for you.
Let me be full, let me be empty.
Let me have all things, let me have nothing.

I freely and heartily yield all things to your pleasure and disposal.
And now, O glorious and blessed God,
Father, Son and Holy Spirit, you are mine, and I am yours.
So be it.
And the covenant which I have made on earth,
let it be ratified in heaven.
Amen.

A daily prayer (author unknown)

O, Jesus, meek and humble of heart,
Hear me, deliver me Jesus:
From the desire of being loved,
From the desire of being extolled,
From the desire of being honoured,
From the desire of being praised,
From the desire of being preferred to others,
From the desire of being consulted,
From the desire of being approved,
From the fear of being humiliated,
From the fear of being despised,
From the fear of suffering rebuke,
From the fear of being wronged,
From the fear of being suspected.
And. Jesus, grant me grace to desire:

That others might be loved more than I,
That others may be esteemed more than I,
That in the opinion of the world, others may increase, and I decrease,
That others may be chosen, and I set aside,
That others may be praised, and I unnoticed,
That others may be preferred to me in everything,
That others may be holier than I, provided I become as holy as I should.90

Prayer based upon the testimony of an unknown African martyr for Christ

Lord,
Because of You, my past is redeemed, my present makes sense and my future is secure.
By Your grace, I'm done with low living, sight walking, small planning colourless dreams, tamed visions, mundane talking, cheap living and dwarfed goals:
May I no longer seek pre-eminence, prosperity, positions, promotions, or popularity; to be right, first, tops, recognized, praised, regarded or rewarded.

May I now live by faith, lean on Your presence, walk with patience, pray without ceasing and labour with power, for my face is set, my goal is Heaven, my road is narrow and my way is rough.

Though my companions are few, my Guide is reliable and my mission clear.

Because of You, I cannot be bought, compromised detoured, lured away, turned back, deluded or delayed.

With Your help, I will not flinch in the face of sacrifice, hesitate in the presence of adversary, negotiate at the table of the enemy, ponder at the pool of popularity or meander in the maze of mediocrity.

Never allow me to give up, shut up or let up; until I have stayed up, stored up, prayed up, paid up and spoken up for the cause of Christ.

For I am yours— a disciple of the Lord Jesus Christ. AMEN

Endnotes

1 F. W. Krummacher, *Sifted Silver*, compiled by John Blanchard (Darlington: Evangelical Press), 318.

2 J. F. X. O'Conor, *A Study of Francis Thompson's Hound of Heaven* (New York: John Lane, 1921), 7.

3 C. S. Lewis, *Surprised by Joy: the Early Shape of My Life* (San Diego: Harcourt Brace Jovanovich, 1984), 228–229.

4 Pierre-Joseph Proudhon, quoted in Karl Lowith, *Meaning in History: the Theological Implications of the Philosophy of History* (Chicago: University of Chicago Press, 1949), 63.

5 Ray Comfort, 'Our Conscience' in Daily Evidence blog, August 24, 2016. https://dailyevidence.wordpress.com/2016/08/24/our-conscience. (Ray Comfort is an evangelist and Founder of Living Waters)

6 James Boice, *Acts: an Expositional Commentary* (Grand Rapids: Baker Books, 1997), 10.

7 Alice Cooper, Interview in *Sunday Times Magazine*, September 2001.

8 Warren Wiersbe, *On Being a Servant of God* (Nashville: Thomas Nelson, 1993), 3.

9 Phillips Brooks, *The Joy of Preaching* (Grand Rapids: Kregel, 1989), 184.

10 C. S. Lewis, *The Weight of Glory* (London: Harper Collins, 2013), 45–6.

11 George F. Dempster, *Finding Lives for Christ* (Basingstoke: Marshall Pickering, 1985), Foreword.

12 Robert Capon, *The Astonished Heart* (Grand Rapids: Eerdmans, 1996), 6.

13 Mike Yaconelli, *Dangerous Wonder* (Colorado Springs: NavPress, 1998), 23–24.

14 Geraint Fielder, *Grace, Grit and Gumption* (Fearn, Ross-shire: Christian Focus, 2000), Back cover.

15 Elizabeth Elliot, *Shadow of the Almighty* (Bromley: STL Books, 1979), 59.

[16] Roger Carswell, *And Some Evangelists* (Fearn, Ross-shire: Christian Focus, 2000), 113.

[17] Warren Wiersbe, *The Wiersbe Bible Commentary: New Testament* (Colorado Springs: David C. Cook, 2007), 334.

[18] Geraint Fielder, *Grace, Grit and Gumption* (Fearn, Ross-shire: Christian Focus, 2000), 184.

[19] Alexander Moody Stuart, quoted in David McIntyre, *The Hidden Life of Prayer* (Fearn, Ross-shire: Christian Focus, 2010), 18.

[20] William Wade, *The Gospel Ministry of Philip the Evangelist* (Leominster: Day One Publications, 2016), 34.

[21] Elizabeth Peabody, *Primary Education* (London; Swan Sonnenschein, 1916), 190.

[22] John Wesley, *The Journals of John Wesley*, abridged by Christopher Idle (Tring: Lion Publishing, 1986), 76 (Journals June 8th 1741).

[23] Michael Green, *I Believe in the Holy Spirit* (London: Hodder & Stoughton, 1984), 68.

[24] I was further encouraged by noting our courtroom encounter recorded by Mr S. in the final chapter of his autobiography (Peter Stringfellow, *King of Clubs* (London: Little, Brown, 1996), 327).

[25] John William Burgon, *Inspiration and Interpretation: Seven Sermons Preached Before the University of Oxford* (Oxford: Parker, 1861), 89.

[26] Steve Levy, *Bible Overview* (Fearn, Ross-shire: Christian Focus, 2008), 10.

[27] Michael Reeves and Tim Chester, *Why the Reformation Still Matters* (London: IVP, 2016), 48–49, 114.

[28] John Wesley, *Standard Sermons* (London: Epworth, 1961), Preface.

[29] Rebecca Manley Pippert, *Out of the Saltshaker* (Nottingham: IVP, 2011), 169.

[30] Paul Williams, *Intentional: Evangelism That Takes People to Jesus* (Leyland: 10 Publishing/Union, 2016), 41.

[31] J. I Packer, *Keep in Step with the Spirit* (Grand Rapids: Baker Book House, 2005), 57.

[32] Paul Williams, *Intentional: Evangelism That Takes People to Jesus* (Leyland: 10 Publishing/Union, 2016), 61.

[33] Zack Eswine, *Kindled Fire* (Fearn, Ross-shire: Christian Focus, 2006), 151.

[34] William Booth, quoted in Warren Wiersbe, *The Wiersbe Bible Commentary: New Testament* (Colorado Springs: David C. Cook, 2007), 788.

[35] Ian Paisley, 'Biographical Sketch' in W. P. Nicholson, *Sermons by W. P. Nicholson* (Belfast: Ambassador Publications, 1982), 4–5.

[36] John Blanchard, *Gathered Gold*, compiled by John Blanchard (Darlington: Evangelical Press, 1984), 119.

[37] C. H. Spurgeon, 'Gospel Missions: a Sermon Delivered on Sabbath Morning, April 27, 1856'. In 'The New Park Street Pulpit', reproduced in 'The Spurgeon Archive': spurgeon.org/sermons/0076.php.

[38] C. H. Spurgeon, *Lectures to My Students*. Lecture 3 (Grand Rapids: Baker Book House, 1980), 47

[39] J. I. Packer, *Evangelism and the Sovereignty of God* (Leicester: IVP, 1979), 11.

[40] Arthur W. Pink, *The Sovereignty of God*. Kindle edition, location 713.

[41] Charles Simeon, *Horae Homileticae*, Preface, i.xvii-xviii. Quoted in J. I Packer, *Evangelism & the Sovereignty of God*. New ed. (Nottingham : IVP, 2010), 20-21.

[42] John Wesley, *Wesley's Journals*, December 20th 1784.

[43] J. I. Packer, *Evangelism and the Sovereignty of God* (Leicester: IVP, 1979), 18–19.

[44] C. H. Spurgeon, 'Why Some Seekers are Not Saved' In *Spurgeon's Sermons*, vol. 41, 1895 [Preached Lord's Day Evening 8th May 1887 on Isaiah 59:1–2].

[45] Lewis Drummond, *Spurgeon Prince of Preachers* (Grand Rapids: Kregel, 1992), 573.

[46] John Wesley, *The Works of John Wesley*, vol. 8 (Grand Rapids: Baker Book House, 1996), 336

[47] Iain Murray, *Wesley and the Men Who Followed* (Edinburgh: Banner of Truth, 2003), 60.

[48] Robert Sheehan, 'God's Love to the Non-Elect.' *Reformation Today* 145 (May/June 1995), 13.

[49] Ibid., 17.

[50] Ibid., 16.

[51] John Nelson. Quoted in Iain Murray, *Wesley and the Men Who Followed* (Edinburgh: Banner of Truth, 2003), 62.

[52] Iain Murray, *Wesley and the Men Who Followed* (Edinburgh: Banner of Truth, 2003), 62.

[53] Helen Roseveare, 'Testimony of Revival'. Recorded at Heath Evangelical Church, Cardiff, 1996.

[54] J. I. Packer, 'Introduction'. In David F. Wells, *God the Evangelist* (Grand Rapids: Eerdmans, 1987), xiv.

[55] A. W. Tozer, *The Set of the Sail* (Chicago: Wing Spread Publishers, 2009), 50–53.

[56] Mark Dever, *Nine Marks of a Healthy Church*, 16

[57] Mrs Howard Taylor, *The Triumph of John and Betty Stam* (London: China Inland Mission, 1935), 98–99.

[58] William Wade, *The Gospel Ministry of Philip the Evangelist* (Leominster: Day One Publications, 2016), 61.

[59] John Ortberg in H. Oral Roberts, *Wounded Warriors of Time* (Bloomington USA: AuthorHouse, 2015), Foreword.

[60] Rebecca Manley Pippert, *Out of the Saltshaker* (Nottingham: IVP, 2011), 18.

[61] Roy Joslin, *Urban Harvest* (Darlington: Evangelical Press, 1982), 79.

[62] John Wesley, *The Journal of John Wesley* (Chicago: Moody Press, 1951), 169.

[63] Amy Carmichael, *Fragments That Remain* (.London: SPCK, 1987), 22–23.

[64] Oswald Chambers, *Shade of His Hand* (Grand Rapids: Discovery House, 2015). Kindle ed., location 1584.

[65] Kent and Barbara Hughes, *Liberating Ministry from the Success Syndrome* (Wheaton: Crossway Books, 2008), 30.

[66] Lawrence Singlehurst, *Sowing, Reaping and Keeping* (Leicester: Crossway Books, 1995), 10–12.

[67] John Piper, 'Beyond Forgiveness: Blasphemy Against the Spirit'. Sermon preached April 1 1984. (Desiring God website: http://www.desiringgod.org/messages/beyond-forgiveness-blasphemy-against-the-spirit).

[68] Michael Reeves, *Christ Our Life* (Milton Keynes: Paternoster, 2014), 73.

[69] Jonathan Edwards, *The Works of Jonathan Edwards*. Vol. 13, The Miscellanies (New Haven: Yale University Press, 1994), 163–164.

[70] C. S. Lewis, *Letters to an American Lady* (Grand Rapids: Eerdmans, 1967), 11 (1 August 1953).

[71] Jonathan Edwards, *A Narrative of Surprising Conversions*. In The Works of Jonathan Edwards. Vol.1 (Edinburgh: Banner of Truth, 1979), 348.

[72] Sherwood Elliot Wirt and Kersten Beckstrom, *Living Quotations for Christians* (New York: Harper & Row, 1974), 266.

[73] Roger Carswell, *Evangelistic Preaching* (Leyland: 10Publishing, 2015), 24–26.

[74] D. Martyn Lloyd Jones, *The Sovereign Spirit* (Wheaton: Harold Shaw, 1986), 89–90.

[75] William Wade, *The Gospel Ministry of Philip the Evangelist* (Leominster: Day One, 2016), 29.

[76] Mark Patterson, Primal: *A Search For the Lost Soul of Christianity* (Colorado Springs: Multnomah Books, 2009), 141–142.

[77] D. Martyn Lloyd-Jones, *Spiritual Depression: Its Causes and Cures* (London: Marshall Pickering 1998), 81).

[78] Allen M Baker, 'Grieving, Quenching and Insulting the Holy Spirit' (Banner of Truth website, 22 April 2014: https://banneroftruth.org/uk/resources/articles/2014/grieving-quenching-insulting-holy-spirit/).

[79] C. T. Studd. In Norman Grubb, *Fool and Fanatic* (Gerrards Cross: WEC, 1980), inside front cover.

[80] C. H. Spurgeon, 'Christian Resignation'. (Sermon delivered early 1859, intended for reading February 24, 1901). (Christian Classics Ethereal Library. Spurgeon'sSermons, vol. 47: 1901).

[81] Mike Yaconelli, Dangerous Wonder (Colorado Springs: NavPress,1998), 14–15.

[82] Ibid., 16.

[83] Oswald J. Smith, *The Passion for Souls* (London: Marshall, Morgan & Scott, 1979), 108.

[84] Simon Guillebaud, *For What it's Worth* (Oxford: Monarch Books, 2006), 14–15.

[85] Anita Mathias, 'Dreaming Beneath the Spires: Anita Mathias's Blog on Faith and Art'. May 2010: 'Helen Roseveare's Great Questions—Is it Worth it? Is Jesus Christ Worth it?' http://anitamathias.com/2010/05/17/helen-roseveare-is-it-worth-it

[86] Phil Callaway, 'Helen Roseveare: Is it Worth it?' In *Servant Magazine*. Reproduced on Laugh Again' website: http://www.philcallaway.ab.ca/Articles/Interviews/HelenRoseveare.htm

[87] Amy Carmichael, *Towards Jerusalem* (London: Triangle, 1987), 85.

[88] (*Blaze* The Official Publication of Flame Ministries International Publication 2011)

[89] Bill Hybels, *Just Walk Across The Room: Four Sessions on Simple Steps Pointing People to Faith* (Grand Rapids: Zondervan, 2006), 20.

[90] Quoted in: George Verwer, *Hunger for Reality* (Carlisle: OM Publishing, 1977), 29.